Heavenly Es

50 Narrative College Application Essays That Worked

By Janine Robinson

Table of Contents

Introduction   4

Essays By Former Students   9

Essays By Students Not My Clients   123

Acknowledgments   148

INTRODUCTION

The best way to learn to write a college application essay is to read what others have written. That's what I tell all my students. By reading excellent examples of narrative-style essays like these, you quickly can understand why this storytelling style is so effective.

The main reason? You want to read them. Slice-of-life narratives include real-life stories that draw the reader into the essay, and along the way, paint an intriguing picture of what the student is all about.

By relating personal experiences and meaningful moments, the writers reveal how they feel and think, what they care about and their goals and dreams. This is exactly what a college wants to learn about you.

Written by real students, this essay collection also can give you an idea of topics that make the best essays. Many of these writers started the essay process believing they had nothing special that set them apart or would make a winning topic. And as you will see, they were all wrong.

I can almost guarantee that once you read a few of these essays, a light bulb will go off in your head and you will think, "That person wrote her college essay about that random topic, and she got into that amazing college? Wow!"

If you need more proof that narrative essays can help you land in your top-choice schools, check out where the authors of these essays got in: Harvard, UCLA, Penn, NYU, Cornell, USC, Northwestern, UC Berkeley, UC Davis, Cal Poly Obispo (SLO), Carnegie Mellon, U. of Washington, U. of Oregon, Boston University, U. of Arizona, Penn State, U. of Colorado, Tulane, and many more. As well as a slew of terrific liberal arts and other colleges: Smith, Williams, Brown, Boston College, University of San Francisco,

Hendrix, University of Puget Sound, Middlebury, Loyola Marymount, Whitman, Haverford, SCAD, etc.

Need I say more? Seriously, the main reason I list these schools is to help you trust that narrative-style, slice-of-life essays work—even at the most competitive schools.

Although it's slowly changing, many parents, teachers, counselors and other "experts" believed essays needed to be formal, academic and impressive. Now, if any of your future essay helpers try to steer you in the wrong direction, you can use this collection to help them understand what really works and why.

It's pretty simple: When you are trying to write about yourself—and reveal your personality, characters, feelings, thinking, goals, passions and dreams—nothing beats a good story.

How Can These Essays Help You Write Your Own?

You don't have to read hundreds of sample essays. Just skim through this collection, and see which ones catch your eye and read a few. You won't believe some of the unexpected topics in these essays, everything from having two moms to being an in vitro baby to sporting big hips.

Notice how most draw you in with the first couple sentences, and keep you reading all the way through. Pay attention to the parts that make you feel something: happy, sad, concerned, curious, sympathetic, etc. If you relate with the writer, or connect and "get" them on some level, you usually can't help but like that person.

Those are the best ones. Those are the essays you want to write—and can. Trust what you respond to, and see if you can emulate the style, writing devices, structure, and other parts that you liked.

These are some of my favorite essays, but none are perfect. They aren't supposed to be. All have sweet parts that do exactly what a college application essay, or personal statement, is supposed to do: give the reader a peek into what makes the writer unique.

Look closely for what makes them engaging and readable. Copy those ideas and techniques. Do you like the anecdotes (true-life mini-stories) they use for the introductions? Try to craft your own. Do you like a certain topic? See if you can find a similar one from your life. Do you like what they have to say, and how they used casual, natural language to share their ideas, feelings and dreams? Channel that voice in your own writing. Write like you talk.

None of these students just sat down and wrote essays this good. Most had help, whether it was brainstorming a topic or polishing the final draft. At some point, however, it was up to each individual student to sit down and pound out something bad, often really bad, and then re-read it and make improvements—over and over again. This is how all good writers work.

Lessons You Can Learn From These Essays

Any extra effort to infuse a little color, details, insights or stories into an essay almost always improves it. It's better to take a creative chance with your essay than to write something formal and dull.

You will notice that most of the topics were not what you would call "impressive." Mundane (everyday) topics worked best: A kid who liked to bake cakes; a girl who got lost in a big city; a boy who got stuck in a tree; a girl who smiled too much. It's not what you write about, but what you have to say about it.

I have written another short book that helps students write these "slice-of-life" essays using a simple, step-by-step approach. You might be able to figure out how these students came up with their topics, and how they wrote their narrative essays just by reading these samples.

But if you want more guidance, *Escape Essay Hell* (available on my EssayHell.com Web site, and Amazon) spells out how to find your core or defining qualities, and then reveal yourself in your essay using specific narrative (storytelling) writing devices, such as anecdotes, dialogue, sensory details, descriptive writing, metaphors and other techniques. This guide sets out the exact 10 steps that I used to help most of the students who wrote these essays.

How My Analyses of These Essays Can Help You, Too

I offer a brief analysis after each essay explaining why I liked the piece, what worked and why. This is my attempt to help you use these essays to write your own. (Some essays already had student-written titles, but I added ones to those that didn't.)

In my comments, I tried to help you understand how these students arrived at their topics, and what writing techniques they used to present them so effectively. Chances are, this will help you start to figure out what you can write about, too.

The first 40 essays were written over the last couple years by students I worked with on their essays, to varying degrees. Many were from my hometown of Laguna Beach, California. Others I worked with via Skype, the phone and email. The final 10 essays were submitted by students from all over the world in response to an essay contest I held on my blog. Although some of them said they used my blog advice and guidebooks, none of them were my tutoring students directly.

Most of these essays are what I call core essays, in that they were submitted to respond to The Common Application prompts, the University of California prompts, or other prompts that ask for a personal-statement type of essay.

I think these essays are more than just college application essays. They are well-crafted narrative essays that are engaging and interesting to read all on their own. And I'm excited and grateful to share these examples of quality student writing with readers beyond the walls of college admissions.

Happy reading!

Brock Csira
Laguna Beach, CA
University of California, Berkeley, CA

Hang Ups

Dangling about 30 feet above the ground, I looked down on the entire neighborhood park with its rolling hills, vibrant green grass, and multiple tall eucalyptus trees. Buckled tightly in my brand new Diamond Mountain climbing harness, I admired my handiwork.

My old blue-and-black braided climbing rope thrown over a branch held me aloft, while a slipknot I tied while hoisting myself up prevented my descent. After a few minutes, I decided to return to the ground, but realized my knot grew too tight for me to untie. I was stuck.

Ever since my dad taught me the Bowline in second grade, the intricacy of knots has fascinated me. I spent hours mastering the craft, reading every knot book and website I could get my hands on. All my knots usually came in handy. In 8th grade, I won a competition in the Boy Scouts with a square knot, beating the instructor who taught an alternative knot that took longer to tie. A couple years later, I rescued my brother's pickup out of the mud with the unbreakable loop of the Bow Line during one of our off-road adventures. I even returned a stranded rock climber's lifeline by tying a Sheep's Bend between a small piece of paracord and his climbing rope.

Ironically, on the day I got stuck in the tree, I spent all morning trying to finally conquer the biggest and baddest knot of them all: the Monkey's Fist. After at least 50 failed attempts at the step-by-step process, my trusty blue rope finally bore the complex, dense sphere of rope. With a heavy Monkey's Fist on the end of my rope, I could throw an end over any branch.

After hoisting myself into the treetops that day I dangled for several hours due to that hastily tied Slip Knot. When my dad finally returned from work and saw me, he lugged over an extension ladder, and laughed as he untied me from the tangle he inspired years earlier.

When I reflected on this adventure, I realized another irony in the situation: It took a complex knot like the Monkey's First to elevate me into the tree, but a simple Slip Knot stopped me from getting back down. Comparing these knots, I learned that the effort and persistence I invest in a challenge like tying a knot translates into a certain lasting power.

A Slip Knot is extremely easy to tie, but disappears with a quick pull on the rope. However, a Monkey's Fist takes hours to learn and minutes to tie, but is impossible to untie. In so many other parts of my life I have experienced this similar relationship: that the more I try, the more useful and permanent the reward.

I expect that my knot-tying adventures, and the related lessons, even the most embarrassing ones, will help me through any future hang ups I encounter from here on out.

ANALYSIS: When Brock was brainstorming for topic ideas, he knew he had a strong interest in engineering. So we started by thinking of qualities, talents and interests he had that would make him an effective engineer.

One of the qualities was that he was a problem solver. And one of his hobbies was knot tying, which is a form of problem solving. Aha! The next step was to find an example of Brock applying his problem-solving skills in real life.

A great way to find compelling real-life, mini-stories—also called anecdotes—is to think of "a time" you faced a problem. Problems can come in many forms: challenges, obstacles, crises, phobias, idiosyncrasies, life changes, etc. When Brock mentioned the time he got stuck in a tree because of his knot-tying ability, we both knew instantly he had hit upon a hot topic.

When you read this essay, notice how naturally this self-deprecating anecdote and knot metaphor showcase Brock's insightful thinking and engineering prowess—as well as his natural humility.

You don't always need to title your essays, but when you land on a witty one like Brock's "Hang Ups," it only makes it that much better.

Alex Segall
Laguna Beach, CA
University of Oregon, Eugene, OR

Better to be Kind

Every day after school, the first thing I would do was climb the stairs to my dad's bedroom and sit on his bed. He would reach out to me and hold my hand while I told him about my day: if I got a good grade on a paper; if a teacher liked one of my comments in class; or if I did two pirouettes instead of one.

He would smile and tell me how proud he was. Nothing made me happier—except the hope that I was also making him happy.

The reason my dad was there for me almost every day of my life was that he was diagnosed with cancer and homebound since I was an infant. I learned about life from leaning on him and from him leaning on me—especially when my mom abandoned us because she couldn't handle his illness.

I went to him for all of my needs. If I had a problem with a friendship or a relationship, if I was scared of the dark, and especially if I procrastinated on a paper, he would stay up late to help me no matter how sick he felt. In a way, he was my life coach, personal therapist, best friend, and dad all in one.

But at the same time, he leaned on me. By the time I was 10, he could no longer eat. My mom stopped cooking. From then on, we no longer gathered around the dinner table. Not only did I have to learn to cook for myself, but to feed my dad through his feeding tube as well. Then during my freshman year when my mom left us, I took over her responsibilities. I did the laundry, cooking, cleaning, and was my dad's personal nurse.

Last year, after I turned 16, he had to go on oxygen 24 hours a day and was bedridden. I learned to pay bills, shop for a month's worth of groceries without spending more than a hundred dollars, and drove him to his doctor's and physical therapy appointments. I could not have friends sleep over, stay out late, or bake cinnamon pancakes because the smell bothered him. When we had to put our house on the market, I raced home every day and frantically cleaned it for showings.

I never talked to my dad about my own struggles or fears because I did not want to worry him. We were both trying to make each other feel better. My goal each day was to make him smile and relieve his suffering any way possible.

But when he left this earth, I felt like my purpose was gone. I was lost. There was no one at home, no one to stay up late and help me with my schoolwork, no one to help me decide what were the right colleges to apply to or what field or major I should consider. Even though my dad leaned on me for everything, I didn't realize how much I leaned on him until he was gone.

Going back to school after he died was the hardest thing, but his passion for education motivated me to resume my classes and get the best grades I could despite my sadness. My dad put me first, and I put him first. Now I am learning how to put myself first.

I now have a life coach, practice meditation, keep a daily journal, and have guardians who love and guide me. In meditation, I am learning to have empathy and compassion for my mom, but at the same time respect my own needs first.

I still think about my dad all the time, and hear his voice encouraging me with his favorite saying: "It is better to be kind than right." I think my dad would be more proud not only that I am pursuing my college dreams, but that I am learning to take care of myself like he always took care of me.

ANALYSIS: This essay nearly broke my heart. And I know it was very challenging for Alex to condense her story to under a mere 650 words. At first, I tried to encourage her to find a different topic, since her dad had only passed away months earlier and she was still grieving. But it became clear that she had to write about this. Nothing else was so defining in her life; nothing even came close.

The challenge of writing about such a traumatic experience was to keep the main point about herself. The objective of a college app essay is to reveal your unique qualities and character, and not just tell a poignant story, especially about someone else. Alex did a great job of relaying what happened to her dad and herself so we felt the impact, but mainly focusing on how it affected her.

She gave the essay a sharp focus by extracting one part of their complicated relationship—how they each supported the other—and starting the piece with a moving example (anecdote) of how that worked. Also, despite the tragedy of his death, Alex did not allow the reader to feel sorry for her, and kept the message positive and hopeful—just like she is.

Brooks Johnson
Laguna Beach, CA
Loyola Marymount University, Los Angeles, CA

Call Me Crazy

After two hours of intense racing on the open water, we thought our day was done. Instead, our coach ordered us to race another five miles home, rowing as hard as when we came. Stuck in the middle of the harbor with seven other teammates in the crew boat, there was nowhere to hide.

"Give me a reason to call 911," coach yelled. Drained and exhausted, I could feel my eyes starting to close. Tunnel vision set in. For a few moments, I blacked out.

I had been here before. This was the point where I had to push my body to do the opposite of what my brain wanted me to do: Go even harder. I focused on the coxswain yelling at me, and hoped my adrenaline wouldn't wear off.

When I first joined the team as a freshman, I only knew a little about this sport. My older brother warned me about the ridiculous hours and tough workouts. The one thing no one told me, though, is that to row crew you had to be a little crazy. It's not the mentally insane type of crazy, but the type where you force yourself to disregard all logic and reason and push yourself to keep going.

After four years of rowing crew, I realized that this was exactly what I loved. This zone that I get into allowed me to break down new mental and physical boundaries every day. It gave me the satisfaction of knowing I went harder than any other previous day.

I never even knew I had this type of mindset until I started crew. Not only did this bring out my new mindset, but it grew each day. Every day I looked forward to pushing myself to my limits—and then climbing down deeper into that well to exceed my prior limits.

When I first started crew, my coach encouraged me to go into what he called our "dark place." This "dark place" was where my mind retreated when I was in extreme pain while rowing. Knowing that it was only my mind holding me back from going any harder, I learned to reverse my thinking so I almost craved the pain to make myself go faster.

It wasn't until recently that I realized how much crew shaped my life and how I've changed over the course of it. My intensity, drive, but mainly the nature of my competiveness has been somehow honed, sharpened and brought to light for me.

Now, when I'm supposed to stop, or feel something is trying to hold me back, all I want to do is push harder to break through it. Now, if I didn't do well on a test, I challenged myself to do better on my next one by doing whatever it took to prepare, and then some extra on top of that. I've also started using the idea from crew where the top guys push the bottom guys to spur a competitive collaborative environment in my classes and with friends.

While I'm conscious of this internal competiveness almost all of the time, I don't feel crazy. I feel motivated and empowered. Even when we raced back on fumes after that grueling workout in the harbor, I couldn't believe how invigorated and strong I felt once back on land. As we brought in the boats, my teammates and I re-capped the painful details, laughing at the same time. None of us could wait for the next day to break another barrier. Call us crazy. We like it that way.

ANALYSIS: When I met with Brooks to brainstorm a topic idea for his Common App essay, he wanted to write about his passion for crew. I kept warning him how sports-themed

16

essays are often dull and cliché. But he kept pushing to write about crew. And it's a good thing he did!

This essay showed me that you can write about anything— even the topics that are often flagged as overdone or potentially boring to read (sports, mission trips, pets, etc.). I still believe you need to be careful of those topics, and that the key is to find something interesting that happened within those topics. Brooks essay is not just about crew, but how those punishing practices re-shaped his DNA.

His essay didn't just say how he learned to work harder or be self-disciplined; his essay showed how he had to be a little crazy. It was critical that Brooks had a clear idea of his main point with this essay before he started writing it so it didn't fall into the traps of writing about sports.

Once he focused on the crazy quality of crew, Brooks was able to brainstorm a real-life example to craft into an anecdote for his introduction. He re-created it by setting the scene (on the open water) with details (five miles home; tunnel vision; blacked out; coxswain yelling…) and dialogue ("Give me a reason to call 911.").

Brooks didn't tell us how crazy he had to be to row crew. Instead, he just shared one example and we got it immediately. You felt his pain. Then he hit us with the unexpected: He not only endured this craziness, he loved it.

Dylan Somerset
Laguna Beach, CA
Boston University, Boston, MA

Window Dressing

Standing by the display window, I wrapped my arms around Sarah's slippery waist, struggling as I pulled the sheer, black turtleneck over one arm. As I yanked the sweater over her other arm, I heard a snap. One of her fingers dropped to the ground.

Although Sarah and the store's other two mannequins were both relatively new, it has always been a battle to constantly change the mannequins and keep them fashionable. Needless to say, I was not looking forward to the skinny jeans.

But, I knew that working at this small boutique in my hometown presented a unique opportunity for me. Adrift, a tiny but hip clothing store for women, gave me a taste of the competitive fashion industry that I love. As a high school junior, I felt lucky for the challenge to create the seasonal displays and transform the mannequins.

Even as I wrestled the mannequins in the store window as passersby gaped and laughed, I enjoyed learning about how to style them in eye-catching outfits. During the two years I worked at Adrift, I jumped at every chance to learn more about the latest fashion trends, and also to understand what drove the business of sales and retail.

When I was first hired, I mainly worked alongside the manager, but after several months my devotion to the job became evident. I received new responsibilities. No matter how intimidated I felt with these unfamiliar tasks, I always tried to dive in with enthusiasm and confidence.

To my surprise, I loved even the most arduous roles. The folding and steaming of clothes, the reorganization of the store, and even the hours of inventory, taught me more about the industry.

My dedication to the menial tasks paid off. Last July the owner invited me to the Los Angeles Market to help merchandise the store. We spent almost that entire day walking around to all the different designers' show rooms and previewing their collections. I felt so fortunate to participate in the buying process, and that my opinion was valued.

The owner of the store also allowed me to explore a new way of marketing by starting and managing the Adrift Facebook page. Facebook was something the owner did not know much about, and that was where my age gave me an advantage. With the Facebook page, I was able to reach out to all different age groups and market our small store.

As summer ends and fall begins my ongoing battle with the mannequins continues—it's off with the bikinis and back on with the sweaters and jeans. I have learned to laugh with those people who walk past me on the sidewalk and stare as I wrestle with the mannequins.

My increased responsibilities have only increased my creativity, my business sense, and my love of fashion. I believe that all my skills that I have learned at Adrift boutique will prove beneficial to a hopefully life long career in the fashion industry.

ANALYSIS: Dylan's essay is an example of how jobs can make great college app essay topics. Writing about a job almost always reveals a student who is industrious and hardworking right off the bat. What college wouldn't love those qualities?

Also, the nature of most first jobs students take in their teens are humble by nature, and the learning curve is big (and sometimes entertaining) as well.

My favorite part of Dylan's essay is her sense of humor. She does a terrific job of setting the scene by describing herself in the window so we can almost visualize her changing the awkward mannequin as passersby gawked at her.

I don't know if she meant to do this, but withholding some of the details—that Sarah wasn't a real person—gave her introduction a suspenseful quality.

Dylan didn't set out to write a funny essay, but this description can't help but make us laugh. There's something powerful about showing yourself in a vulnerable moment. It makes you come across as very likable, in my opinion.

She starts by describing one challenging (and amusing) moment during her job, and then goes on to expand about the nature of her job and what she learned. One point of her essay was to show that her job had its unique demands, and at times was taxing, but that she realized how much she had to learn by sticking with it.

Duncan Lynd
Laguna Beach, CA
California State University, Long Beach, CA

A Small World

While grabbing lunch between games at a water polo tournament, I noticed one of my new teammates rarely looked me in the eye. Instead of taking the empty seat next to me, he opted to sit across the table. Even when I tried to start a conversation with him, he only looked down, and mumbled, "Oh, hey," and walked away.

This type of cold-shoulder treatment wasn't new to me. I'm a big guy. In bare feet, I'm about 6 feet 7 inches tall, and I'm pushing 300 pounds. Yes, it can be a pain. I bump my head going through doorways, I don't fit in most mid-size cars, and I can barely squeeze into most classroom desks. But I understand that the world is made for average-sized people, and I like to think I'm above average. One thing, however, is hard for me to take: People who don't know me assume I'm mean.

Like my frosty water polo teammate. I understand why he was intimidated by me, especially since he was one of the smaller players. I would have felt the same way. When I meet people for the first time, I often draw conclusions or make assumptions. Almost all my life, I've had to deal with the expectations and judgments people make about me just because I'm often the largest kid in the room. Ever since I was a kid there has been pressure for me to perform athletically because of my size and strength.

When I went to grocery store, random people consistently asked me if I played football. When I told them, "No," the men always lectured me not only about why I should play football, but what I should be doing with my life, with my body, and with my potential. I normally just nodded and smiled, but it bothered me that they thought they knew what was best for me.

Not only did I never play football, but I defied many of the assumptions people made about me. How many people my size love nothing more than mixing up a chocolate batter, and decorating a three-layer cake? Beside my passion for baking, I also love working with little kids. For the last two summers, I volunteered at a camp where I taught kids how to surf. My nickname was Teddy Bear. And if I wanted to make my friends fall on the ground laughing, I reminded them of my dream to learn to play the violin.

In general, I ignore what people say to me or think about me when it comes to my size. Instead of reacting, I usually just give them a smile. On many levels, there are advantages to towering over most of the world. I always get the front seat since I don't fit in the back. No one even dares call "shotgun." I usually have the best seat in the house, whether it's a rock concert or a ball game, no matter where I sit. And if people are getting rowdy and making my friends uncomfortable, all I need to do is step in the middle and simply ask, "What's going on?" and they disperse.

Even the people who are intimidated at first by me eventually come around once they get to know me. Like the water polo player at the restaurant. Within about two weeks, we finally had a conversation and ended up finding we had a lot in common. In fact, he ended up as my best friend. For me, it is a small world after all, but I wouldn't have it any other way.

ANALYSIS: How can you not like this guy after reading his essay? When I met with Duncan, it was obvious that his impressive stature could make a nifty essay topic. On some level, it had to define him. But we didn't want it to be predictable or cliché.

Many students have traits or idiosyncrasies that feel unique to them, but the truth is many other students share them, such as being a big guy, being super tall, having too many freckles, being clumsy, afraid of heights, etc. They can all make terrific topics, but you have to work a little harder to give them a twist or something unexpected.

After talking about his height and girth a bit, it came out that not only did he bump his head a lot, but that people made assumptions about him based on his difference. Bingo! That other kids thought he was mean just because he was big was a different twist on the idea of being large.

By sharing how this bothered him, Duncan revealed himself as a sensitive, empathetic and insightful guy. That is all great stuff! You don't only want to share your stories, but also how they make your feel, what you think and learn from them. Then you will have a knock-out essay.

Ava Eastman
Laguna Beach, California
University of Colorado, Boulder, CO

My Little Secret

When my friend texted me that she was already at my front door for our study group, I leaped up onto my bed. In one pass, I ripped down the giant poster of Robert Patterson gazing out above my pillow, shooting pushpins in every direction.

Next, I scrambled over to my desk, and snatched the Edward and Bella dolls, pristine in their unopened plastic cases, and tossed them behind the couch. Finally, in one swoop, I gathered the pictures, buttons, cards, books and other Twilight Saga memorabilia off my shelf and buried them deep inside my sock drawer.

Moments before my friend burst into my room, I made one last glance for any overlooked signs of my deep dark secret: I am a Twilight junkie. I have every DVD, CD, doll, book, shirt, poster—you name it. I've seen the movies at least 4 times, including the midnight premier of each movie. I've read the books so many times I can quote from my favorite scenes. As much as I love these characters, no one has a clue about my obsession.

This Twilight mania is very unlike me. I enjoy reading novels like *Crime and Punishment, Jane Eyre, Of Human Bondage*—classic literature, not some mainstream teenage girl fantasy romance book. And I am not a softy. I aspire to be a chemical engineer. I balance three part time jobs. I have a realistic outlook on life, and I will persevere through any obstacles I face.

The last thing I want to be considered is "mainstream." I enjoy being that girl who is a chemistry nerd and a modern dancer, who loves photography, and plays tennis recreationally. I consider myself an individual, someone who refuses to fit neatly into any group or classification. In fact, I pride myself in stepping up even in the face of conventional thinking to voice my thoughts and opinions. I don't mind being the odd one out, if it's something I believe. I'm a leader. However, there is something about this book that touches my soft side.

Twilight offers me a world of fantasy to escape the demands of real life. Although I work best under pressure, the Twilight books offer me a break from the pressure and a place where I can get lost in my imagination. I strive to be an individual, but part of me feels comforted that Twilight can unite me with millions of other girls around the country who have fallen in love with the same guy, the same fantasy.

Despite my fierce exterior, I do enjoy dreaming about a world where a person can fall in love with something as ghastly as a vampire. Maybe despite all our efforts to be individuals, we all share the same values, such as love, and even passion. Twilight offers an escape for me. But still, no one can ever know about my obsession. To the world, I'm unique and fierce. This is just between you and me.

ANALYSIS: This is one of my favorite essays. When we brainstormed Ava's defining qualities in search of topic ideas, it quickly became clear that she was a high-achiever on many fronts. The quality we chose to explore was "fierce." But Ava didn't write about how fierce she was; instead she wrote about an opposite quality that she rarely showed. Her soft side.

It amazed me how perfectly this approach worked. Ava featured one unlikely part of her personality to highlight all the other impressive features in such a natural way. By confessing to her one mainstream interest (the crush on her idol), she was able to play off it and showcase all her other interests that were unconventional and unique.

The confessional nature of the essay also helped Ava come across as likeable and balanced despite her fierce approach to life. It also showed someone who has the confidence and maturity to see herself in an honest way, and admit that even the fiercest people sometimes need a gentle escape.

Her playful ending nailed the essay. Her tone throughout the essay was light and familiar, and it was almost as if she ended the essay with a wink.

Reece Barton
Laguna Beach
New York University, New York, NY

Trash Talk

On our way to get fish tacos, about eight blocks from my house, I spotted the sign out of the corner of my eye. "Stop the car!" I shouted. Blake slammed on the brakes and threw the car into reverse. My eyes hadn't deceived me, the hand-written sign read: "Free Trampoline."

Ever since I can remember, I have loved turning other people's trash into my personal treasures. I cannot walk past a garage sale without digging through the neighbor's junk. Over the years, I have even decorated my room with accessories from various sales and giveaways.

I scored my giant box television from a church sale, towed my slipcovered couch home from my neighbor's yard sale, and rescued old-school street signs that decorate my walls from my grandma's trash. So, when I saw the sign for a free trampoline, I knew I had to make it mine.

To most, a 10-year-old trampoline wouldn't be worth dragging home, but to me, it was almost too good to be true. By bribing my friends with free tacos, I convinced them to follow the sign leading to the trampoline, and we pulled up to the house. Ahead of us were three flights of stairs up to the backyard. I jumped out of the car and, scared that someone might beat me to the front door, I sprinted up the stairs.

After what seemed like an eternity, a man answered the door. Out of breath, I asked if the trampoline was still available. "Yeah, it's out back," he said, pointing out beyond a glass door. I nearly dropped to my knees with joy.

Even though the trampoline wasn't in the best shape, it was much bigger than I imagined and all the necessary parts were there. "The deal is, if you can take it apart and out of my house, you can have it," the man called up. My jaw hit the floor. I couldn't believe this could be mine for next to nothing.

After two hours of dissembling it piece by piece, my friends and I wrestled and rolled it down the stairs, finally hoisting it onto the roof of my friend's Jetta. We didn't have any rope, so four of us walked alongside the car, supporting each corner of the trampoline all eight blocks back to my house. Drivers honked and shouted at us, but it didn't slow us down. Within an hour we had it assembled in my backyard, and we were soon lounging on the trampoline, chowing down on fish tacos.

Sometimes, I surprise myself by how far I will go to hunt down a good deal. To me, however, the deal is just the beginning. I love creating useful things out of other people's junk.

Just last week, I built a shelving system out of some scrap wood and mini-fans for my friend that was moving to college. Last winter, I made a makeshift bobsled out of two old snowboards and shopping cart wheels. I've learned that things don't lose their value after a few years of wear and tear. My neighbors' trash literally is my treasure.

ANALYSIS: If you had to pick what quality Reece was trying to showcase about himself in this essay, what would you guess? The guy loves to find junk and turn it into private treasures. But what does this say about his personality or character?

I love how it reveals a couple genuine qualities, and the main one is that he is resourceful. Besides hauling home a free trampoline, Reece thinks independently and decides what has value or not. And then he goes after it with zeal.

The other qualities Reece reveals about himself simply by relating this "time" he lugged home a free trampoline is that he is clearly self-assured and determined, and also scrappy in how he figured out how to get it home.

My favorite line is how he makes the comment that he sometimes surprises even himself. It's as though he has never really stopped and thought about what drives his passion for other people's cast-offs. And to me, that only makes him all the more likable.

Gabrielle Mark Bachoua
San Diego, CA
University of California, Davis, CA

Leaping Dancer

As my mom backs out of our driveway, I glance at the back seats to make sure my basketball gear is there, along with my schoolbooks, phone charger, and beat-up copy of *Catch-22*. We slowly wind through my neighborhood and over about a half dozen speed bumps, then pull onto the highway heading south with the other Sunday traffic.

I sit back and watch the familiar landmarks—the large Denny's sign with the missing "N," the short stretch of undeveloped land, the Shell billboard that meant we were almost there—flash past my window.

I've made this 20-mile trip between my parents' homes for the last decade, four times a week, ever since they divorced when I was seven. I must have taken it more than a thousand times. Sometimes I dreaded getting into that car, and resented my parents for putting my older sister and I through the circular logic that moving us back and forth will make our lives normal because we see each parent often, but moving back and forth isn't normal, unless they make it normal, which isn't normal. Now I know it makes sense because normal isn't ideal, normal is the unexpected and the crazy and the unforgiving.

 I now realize that those rides are the consistency amidst the madness. Looking out the window and down to the lane reflectors I think... about how on Friday's basketball game my jump shot was off because I was floating to the left, about how I'm excited to see my dog and cat, about how upset I am because of Yossarian's predicament, about how I'll miss my dad, about how veterinary medicine is fascinating, about how I needed to study for my chemistry

30

test, about how I will work harder to get into my dream school, and about how I'm glad that I get to take a nice nap before I go to mom's.

I even remember the first time years ago when I noticed the smudge on the rear driver's side window, which was shaped into a leaping dancer—a dancer in white. I would watch her move through the trees in El Cajon Valley, bob my head up and down to help her jump over hillside terraces of Spring Valley, and keep her from crashing into the Westfield mall sign two miles from my mom's home.

It was those hours I spent thinking silently to myself when I learned more about who I am, where I envision myself going, and what my role is in this world. Sitting in the front seat, I'd take a moment to look back to see that same dancer in white, however faceless, nameless, and abstract, gave me a sense of comfort. That even though I wasn't really 'home', I still was, because home isn't simply where you rest your head, but also where you have the security to dream inside of it.

ANALYSIS: Once again, an essay like this proves that you can pick almost anything to write about as long as you give it a focus. In this case, Gabrielle picked a simple stretch of roadway between her parent's homes. She described the weekly routine and drive with vivid, descriptive details, so you felt as though you were in the car staring out the same window.

But she used the trip as a metaphor for a meaningful time in her life, when she had lots of downtime to reflect on her life, her feelings and dreams. Even though it shares the pain of her parent's divorce in an understated way, that's always in the background—and we can tell it has shaped her.

If she never had the time to daydream and reflect on her day, who knows how she would have been different somehow, or those emotions would have played out somewhere else.

Nothing really happens in this essay, but it still manages to have momentum and hold our interest. I love how she personifies a little smudge on the window into a dancer, another metaphor for her own journey.

In the end, Gabrielle explored the idea of home, and defined it more as a journey than a destination—whether riding in a car for a commute between houses or a lifelong adventure.

I believe Gabrielle didn't set out to write a "deep" essay filled with metaphors and heavy insights, but by describing a simple routine and then reflecting upon what it meant to her, she revealed herself as an observant, reflective and wise young woman.

Jack Wyett
Laguna Beach, CA
University of Southern California, Los Angeles, CA

Sisters

It was the middle of the day, and I was relaxing on the big couch in the family room, happily watching the last few minutes of a potential buzzer beater game. First, my oldest sister walked in, following by the other two with their friends.

"Get out," my youngest sister demanded, standing in front of the screen.

I knew right then, that all the begging I could do wouldn't get her to budge, or the entire group to leave me alone. But I always gave it a try.

"I'm not leaving," I said, sinking deeper into the couch. After that, they launched into their threats and other attempts to push me out of their girl world.

Ever since I can remember, my three older sisters did whatever they could to make me get lost. When they were all crammed in the bathroom playing with make-up in front of the big mirror, they would slam the door in my face. Or when they had friends sleep over, they would banish me from their bedrooms. It wasn't that I wanted to join them in their activities, but I was bored and lonely.

The only time they wanted me around was when they needed me to do their dirty work. Like when there was a spider to be caught, who did they call? Me. When there was trash to be picked up, who did they call? Me. When something went wrong, who did they blame? Me.

I was the runt of the family and the lowest rank in the hierarchy. My three sisters, now in their early 20s, were about 5 to 7 years older than me. And up until junior high, they all towered over me. They were never really mean, but loved to tease me constantly. To them, I was "the baby" or "little guy."

But then things changed. By eighth grade, I started sprouting up, growing about a foot in just a couple years. Until 8th grade when all of a sudden everyone started looking at me differently. I had grown taller than everyone and now I was in control. I noticed that along with my new height, my maturity increased and the level of respect that I received from my sisters did as well. The teasing stopped. And we even started to have normal conversations about school and friends. Even my parents started treating me more like a young man than the baby of the family.

Even though I can't say I enjoyed some of those moments, I can say on some level that I understood that treatment since I was just at the bottom of the pecking order. And I also don't feel like I need to get back at them, even though I now have the clear advantage physically. If nothing else, I am more sensitive to people who are at a disadvantage in the world, whether it's because of social status or other circumstances. I know what it's like to be the underdog.

Even though my role in a family dominated by girls changed over the years, I was not completely off the hook. Having to complete the tasks that the younger brother would do never really ended. I still take out the trash, and stomp on spiders. But now when it comes to the last minutes of a Laker's game, I'm not moving.

ANALYSIS: Boy did Jack have a hard time settling on a topic. I know Lynn Fair of Square One counseling spent time brainstorming, and they kept hitting walls. Both of us kept urging him to explore his family because he had the three older sisters. But he was pretty resistant at first.

But once he started describing out loud some of the details of his daily life as the youngest of a family of girls, I believe he began to hear his own story, and voice. This was a perfect topic for the fifth Common App prompt that asks to share a transition into the adult world.

He started with a simple recreation of a typical argument with his sisters. There's nothing impressive or shocking with this topic or anecdote; just a vivid description of normal, bickering siblings: Something many of us can relate with easily. That's what makes it work—the reader connects with the writer's "problem."

And I love his confessions: "I was at the bottom of the pecking order." And, "I know what it's like to be the underdog." And his sense of humor: "I was the runt of the family." By using self-deprecating descriptions of his childhood role, Jack can then show that he is now mature enough to look back and understand what was going on, accept it for what it was, and enjoy his new role without resentment. This reveals a mature, well-adjusted kid with a nice sense of humor. What else could you want?

Luc Stevens
Laguna Beach, CA
University of Oregon, Eugene, OR

Skating Through Hard Times

Six years ago, my family was caught in a terrifying landslide when my home and a dozen others slid down the side of a canyon in Laguna Beach.

I was in fifth grade eating breakfast with my family when the floor of my home gave way under our feet. We barely escaped from the house before it buckled into two pieces, and ran to safety before the entire hillside gave way. Our home was destroyed, and we narrowly escaped with our lives.

Within less than 10 minutes, my life literally fell out from under me. For the next five years, my family moved over a dozen times, often living out of boxes with friends and relatives. Besides my clothes and basic necessities, the only thing I hauled from house to house was my collection of skateboards.

Six months after the landslide, the city of Laguna Beach relocated us to a recycled trailer on a parking lot at the end of town so my parents could save money to rebuild our home. I see it now as an extremely generous gesture but at the time it was difficult. Living in this dilapidated, thin-walled trailer was definitely not the life I had envisioned. My backyard was an enormous parking lot.

As a lifelong skateboarder, however, that flat expanse of asphalt helped me get through the hardest years of my life. You see, I'm a skater from a hillside neighborhood and had never experienced such space and opportunity. I took advantage of the situation and made this neglected, dirty parking lot into a skateboarding oasis with ramps and rails that my friends donated.

36

We would all gather together after school as a release from the pressures of life for a while, practicing trick after trick, working to fine-tune each maneuver. Contests were created, videos shot, and movies made.

For the first time in my life, I had a flat area where my friends and I could hang out. Even though we didn't talk much about the landslide, these friendships were both a distraction and softened the unpleasant living situation.

Also, balancing sports and loads of homework, I turned to what I thought of as my new backyard skate park at night to escape from reality each day. The sense of riding back and forth on a cold night helped me relax and persevere through my studies and life in general.

Numerous years passed in that cramped rickety, old trailer and life wore on dealing with everything from highway noise reverberating right outside our door to the constant rodent problem. When my family's new, hillside home finally came to completion at Christmas last year, I was more than ready to move.

The only thing I would miss from my five-year ordeal was my beloved "skate park." After moving into our permanent home, the crazy life I endured since fifth grade was now over and even though I could not bring the skate ramps themselves, I was able to bring plenty of memories.

One of the most important lessons I learned through all this is that I have the ability to find positive opportunities even in the grimmest circumstances. If I could find friendship, support and fun in a parking lot, I know I can find the upside to almost any situation.

ANALYSIS: Luc almost had no choice but to write about how he and his family lost their home in a landslide when he was young. It was such a defining experience—not just the terrifying event, but the long, slow process of "going home."

I like how Luc recounted briefly the actual slide, and how he didn't over dramatize or dwell on that. Instead, he picked right up on how he turned a bad situation into something positive. Like any good personal essay, this one has a clear universal truth: How every cloud has a silver lining (if you find it.)

Because Luc's description of his experience showed us how bad things were and then the steps he took to improve them, he never had to spend a lot of time explaining what he learned. He only needed a couple sentences at the very end to share his lessons.

A lot of students who grow up in Southern California want to write about their passions for sports, such as surfing and skate boarding. I usually steer them away from these topics, since they aren't very interesting to read. Luc's essay is a huge exception!

Ashlyn Alter
Laguna Beach, CA
University of California, Davis, CA

The In Vitro Life

It's only 60 degrees out, but the first thing my family does when we hit the beach during a summer evening is build a bonfire. Even though I sit as close as possible to the heat, I always get goose bumps and my teeth start to chatter.

I try to scoot closer, my mom yells, "What are you doing?! You need to back up!" Then she goes back to the car and brings me a blanket.

Everyone in my family, and all my close friends, know this quirk about me: I'm always cold. People who first meet me, however, find that I'm an open, bubbly and warm person. I love talking to strangers, I love meeting new people, and above all, I love making others feel comfortable.

But there's a reason I'm wearing a sweatshirt and leggings in August. There's no physical explanation for my coldness. My circulation is fine and I'm in great health. But I've had this problem since I was born—in fact, for three years before I was born. I have a theory. I was conceived through in vitro fertilization. My mom was unable to get pregnant, and after five years trying to conceive, she set aside several eggs. After three years of failed attempts, she delivered my older brother, Cody, while I waited in the egg freezer in the lab. For the next three years, I sat there chilling.

My parents explained all this to me when I was about seven. I got a kick out of the idea that I had a "twin" who was three years older. And it warmed my heart to know how much they wanted me, and the lengths they went to bring me into world. Even though no one believes me, I'm convinced all that time in the freezer somehow permanently lowered my body temperature. And I've been trying to warm up ever since.

39

I may feel cold all the time, but everyone always tell me that I radiate warmth. When I go to work at my job at a home furnishings store called Tuvalu, I always make sure to bring a sweater to endure the air-conditioning. I know little to none about designers, fabrics and vendors, but I excel with customer service.

At Tuvalu, I'm the employee who gets cornered into half-hour conversations with the oldest customers about topics that have little to do with home décor—anything from the key to life or the secrets to making a flakey piecrust. My coworkers try to rescue me from these conversations, but the truth is I enjoy the knowledge of others and the perspectives they give me.

Just this summer, while my friends hung out at the beach, I volunteered to surprise my grandparents, who were recovering from various health issues. My dad said I would "change the energy." It wasn't hard work at all. I walked the dog with my grandmother and listened to my grandfather boast about his new teeth. I loved that I could cheer them up simply with my presence.

Being constantly cold has its set backs, but I think it also helps me generate warmth among those around me. Some people might get ahead in the world by being assertive, ambitious or even hard-edged, but I believe in the value of always caring about the welfare of others. No matter how cold you feel, you can always heat up a room with a friendly hello. But it doesn't hurt to bring a jacket.

ANALYSIS: This is an example of an essay that doesn't take itself too seriously, but does exactly what a personal essay is supposed to do: Give you an idea of what the writer is all about. After reading this essay, we can tell that Ashlyn is a loving, warm person, and she revealed herself in such a delightful, humorous way. (Ashlyn doesn't try to be funny or write a comedic essay—she's actually quite serious—but when she states her opinions and "theories," they just happen to be funny. Note the difference.)

Ashlyn took a risk by asserting something that others might find ridiculous: That she is always cold because she was conceived in vitro and the egg was in a freezer. But she pulled it off perfectly. She did this by stating her "problem" (being cold all the time) and sharing her "theory" as to the cause. Because she qualifies her theory as just that, she could then go onto to use her "big chill" as a way to showcase her warm personality.

Notice how she maintains the right tone throughout the essay, keeping it light and playful with language such as, "I sat there chilling," and, "I've been trying to warm up ever since." This is someone who is in on the joke and doesn't take herself too seriously—what likable qualities. At the same time, Ashlyn shows her wit by playing her literal coldness against her figurative trait of being warm, social and loving.

Alex Amato
Washington, Connecticut
Penn State, Philadelphia, PA

Taking Orders

As I scrambled to drop a check at one table, pour more coffee at another, and get orange juice to a third, I noticed a woman angrily bolt towards the restaurant kitchen. All I could think was, "Oh boy, what now?"

When I headed back to the kitchen to see what was wrong, she handed me an empty plate, yelling about how I mixed up her order with her son's. After what felt like an hour-long conversation with my boss, he agreed to pay for her meal – a party of five. And it was coming straight out of my paycheck.

I was so frustrated I wanted to scream. But I had to finish serving her table, smiling. It took self-control, and I had to swallow my pride – something I despised doing ever since I was a kid.

But over the last year that I waited tables at the upscale restaurant in my hometown, I learned what it meant to grow up. Although some of it was painful, I figured out that it's often about doing the right thing—even when all you want at the moment is the wrong thing.

While waiting tables, I had many opportunities to practice my people skills. I learned the value of patience, how far an optimistic personality goes, and that being a good employee is mainly about having a strong work ethic.

For me, that was the easy part of the job. The most difficult challenge was watching customers take advantage of situations, and being powerless. The customer was always right. That still drives me insane.

42

But I view myself as a goal-oriented person; I trained myself to think about the big picture more than I worry about the instant satisfaction—such as proving a customer wrong. With that demanding woman who wanted a free lunch for her entire family, I felt like shouting at the top of my lungs at her. All she had to do was notice that her food wasn't what she ordered and switch plates with her son.

It was agonizing to watch her manipulate the situation and profit from it – all at my expense. But doing that would certainly destroy my tip from that table, and possibly end up with me getting sent home early that day or even getting fired. I was willing to sacrifice my pride, something I put great value in, in order to make my table happy. So I held my tongue – even though it was painful.

They say it's not always enough to be right. I've learned that that applies to many parts of my life, far beyond waiting tables. It's not all about instant satisfaction; it's about the larger goal. Whether that means putting in that extra hour of studying before an exam, or making the right choice about a party, it's always crucial to have a strong purpose in mind.

That decision marked a huge change in mindset for me. For most of my life, the immediate now was more important than the future. And while I still believe it's important to live every day, it's even more important to think about the future. I believe that mature, farsighted perspective is what separates children from adults.

Whether it's waiting on tables, picking stock investments, or making family decisions, I now like to figure in the larger ramification as best I can. To consider only what brings you instant satisfaction is immature and will serve no purpose. When I see someone like that entitled woman in the restaurant acting like a selfish child, I know I now have the ability to stand back and think and act like an adult.

ANALYSIS: My favorite thing about this essay is that you can almost hear Alex' voice. He showed himself in a powerless situation that drove him crazy, and then related how he dealt with his own tendency to overreact.

He also helped us understand how he not only kept his ego in check, but that he learned a larger life lesson: To look ahead and have a long-term perspective when it comes to decisions.

And he did all this by telling us about "a time" he dealt with an impossible woman at a restaurant and how he unfairly got stuck with her bill. Who couldn't relate to that? We (the reader) could feel his frustration and sense of helplessness in correcting an unfair situation.

This connection makes us care about Alex, so when he goes onto explain what he learned from this experience, we listen and appreciate what he has to say. Alex shared a very human side of himself, and that made him an instant hit—at least with me. And based on his many acceptances, including the top engineering school he plans to attend, with college admissions officers as well.

Ruth Mendoza
Aptos, California
University of California, Riverside, CA

Against the Current

During my break from volunteering at the hospital, I chose to go to my favorite Mexican restaurant by the sea. While sitting next to the window, I looked into the horizon as I saw small waves wash the day's debris onto the moist sand.

As I was taking in the beautiful scenery, an elegant lady motioned me over. Not wanting to be rude, I walked over to her table.

"We're ready to order," she stated, assuming I was a waitress.

While Hollywood constantly portrays Hispanic women as being housemaids or waitresses who often speak incoherent English, the majority of Americans perceive Hispanics as uneducated and don't believe they have the potential to be successful.

I could've been the next Sonia Sotomayor or the next most powerful woman in the United States. Yet because of these stereotypes, I still would've been asked the same question.

Ever since I can remember, it's been tough, if not impossible, to fit into our small town in California. My culture and all the assumptions that go with it, always followed me. My family spoke Spanish at home, we ate enchiladas for dinner instead of pasta, and instead of shopping at our local Safeway store we went to the flea market on Sundays after church to get a *raspado* (frozen ice drink). I felt humiliated when instead of speaking flawless English, I spoke with an accent.

I heard all the grim statistics my entire life: Hispanics live in

45

economic deprivation; they're not as likely to pursue higher education as other races and young Hispanic women are the most likely to get pregnant. As I heard these stereotypes, they began to slowly sink into my brain and haunt me as questions arose. What if I really am not as intelligent as the others? What if I don't have the fortitude to go against the current?

The choice of whether or not to allow being Hispanic be the single barrier that stood between my success and failure rested solely on me. I started to look for opportunities to change patterns, the predictions, and most of all, my self-doubt, in order to prove that we Hispanics, have the ability and potential to be successful.

The fall of my junior year, I started a tutoring group for students who faced oppressive stereotypes in my community. I knew the children deserved a safe place to obtain educational support and feel safe. It became home for many students who felt trapped within the confines of society and a stimulating intellectual environment in which they could get one-on-one help on their homework.

The progress the students made throughout the year was unbelievable. Karen, an English learner who needed extra help with her reading and writing skills, came in not being able to recite the alphabet. Now, she has the ability to write complete sentences. Julissa, another English learner who has learning disabilities, is now able to write complete sentences as well. They are some of the many students who proved that with dedication and perseverance, Hispanics do have the potential to succeed.

Because of our perseverance, the Tutoring Group became so successful that the neighboring church decided to partner with us and expand the program to include other surrounding areas. Now, when I go to college, I know these kids remain in a safe environment and become successful someday.

While misconceptions about Hispanics abound in the nation and we might not be able to change people's perspectives right away, we can work on changing the way we feel about ourselves. Only then, can we get to work changing how others see us.

I learned that with perseverance and dedication, one has the power to enrich lives and become a leader by rising above the status quo. Something that not only I would do all over again if given the chance, but something I would encourage others to do as well.

Now, I am ready to overcome any obstacles and stereotypes on my way to success. Instead of letting them affect me negatively, I will rise and embark on a new journey in which I will prove all those who doubted me wrong.

ANALYSIS: I love Ruth's essay because she showed us her "grit." This is a very powerful quality that colleges, especially, are known to look for in future students. It not only means they have determination, but that they don't give up even under the most oppressive circumstances.

Ruth chose a simple moment from her life to help us stand in her shoes and experience what it feels like to be judged based solely on appearances. This simple anecdote showed us what it might feel like to be discriminated against.

Although she shared the pain and frustration of moments like these, Ruth did not go on to rant and vent her anger. Instead, she explained how she thinks about discrimination, particularly against Hispanics, and vows to fight the stereotypes.

Then Ruth related specific examples of how she had taken steps in her life to reverse some of the patterns of discrimination, and how she helped other students to excel. You can tell by her strong voice that there will be no stopping Ruth in her future efforts to change the world!

Weston Barnes
Laguna Beach, CA
George Mason University, Fairfax, VA

A Swimmingly Good Idea

The shiny goldfish swam circles in my glass of water. "Eat it! Eat it!" my friends chanted at us. When I gulped down the water, the fish tried fighting the current in my throat. I nearly lost it.

The thought of a fish swimming around in my stomach acids freaked me out more than I had anticipated. But I tried not to think about my squirming snack, and instead focused on my goal: I had high hopes for this goldfish stunt.

My plan was to get elected as Laguna Beach High School's Pep Commissioner. Ever since my freshman year, after watching my senior mentor fill the popular position of Pep Commissioner, I knew that I wanted to fill his shoes as a senior.

So last year, my best friend and I decided to run for the most sought-after position in ASB. We knew we had to run a good campaign for the competition was fierce. In order to win the election, we had to display our enthusiastic and creative sides. More importantly, we needed to make sure that the students would not forget us.

All it took was a camera and a computer to put the campaign in full swing. After a few hours of editing the fish footage— adding entertaining commentary and catchy music—we were ready to show the video to the entire school. Not only did we make this campaign video using the fish, we built the whole campaign around this memorable image.

To build anticipation before showing the video, we hung images of goldfish around campus and placed little bowls filled with goldfish in a handful of classrooms. It worked.

Students started asking, "What's the deal with these fish everywhere?" Finally, the video was shown on the morning video announcements to the entire student body. "The goldfish thing really makes sense now," one freshman explained to me. The goal was that anytime someone saw a goldfish, they would think of us. We started the coveted buzz.

As a result of the goldfish and our marketing efforts, we won the election. It wasn't even close. Looking back, I now see that Max and I had turned this fish into a brand; it represented the creativity that we were going to bring the upcoming year. It didn't hurt that we also showed we were passionate enough about winning to swallow a live fish. Through our campaign, I learned that one swimmingly good idea sure can jumpstart a campaign, but how we delivered our message is what helped us win.

ANALYSIS: Just like Weston set out to make himself "unforgettable" in his high school bid for Pep Commissioner, he also made himself memorable by telling that story in this essay. Same goal; same approach; same effect. It worked!

Weston went on to tell us the larger lesson he learned about an area that interested him: business, especially marketing. If it works out, bringing in qualities that link to your future interests, whether in college or beyond, is always a good idea. (Not everyone knows what they want to do, but if you do, why not let colleges know what you got that will make you effective in that field?)

Weston also closed his essay with a memorable last line— using a play on words when he describes his "swimmingly good idea." In these essays, you want to grab the reader with something compelling, and also leave them with a little tidbit they also won't forget. These are called "kicker" lines.

Hannah Clifton
Laguna Niguel, CA
University of Arizona, Tucson, AZ

Walk On

Sitting high on her horse, Molly fiddled with her long brown hair and stuck her fingers in her mouth. Sometimes she would tip to one side, and we would slide her back up into the saddle.

When she got scared or frustrated, Molly would lurch forward, practically lying down on the horse and attempt to bite its neck.

"Molly, make the horse 'walk on'," we instructed her, along with demonstrating how to pat the saddle horn for her special signal to make the horse move forward. We had been trying to teach Molly, a 13-year-old girl who is wheelchair bound from Cerebral Palsy, how to signal commands so she could control her horse for the last couple months.

This time, to our surprise, Molly reached forward and tapped the saddle horn. We all cheered and praised her as we led the horse forward. Even though Molly couldn't respond with words, her body language and her high-pitched shriek let us know how excited she was for herself as well.

In my two years of volunteering at the Shea Therapeutic Riding Center, this moment with Molly was by far the most memorable and rewarding I have ever experienced.

I worked with children and adults with all different kinds of mental and physical disabilities—from Downs Syndrome and Autism to even forms of ADHD. I learned that every rider had their own way of improving their conditions; even small gestures like tapping the saddle to make the horse walk or a simple posture adjustment on their own proves how much control they are gaining over their bodies.

At first, I could never understand the frustration and hardship Molly had to go through on a day-to-day basis. But over time, I understood how all of the kids I worked with at the Shea Center were so strong and so inspiring in their own ways. Recently I suffered a knee injury, which gave me a glimpse of how it might be like without the normal capability of movement and control over my body.

In no way I could ever compare this to the permanent disability Molly and others face, but my setback helped me gain empathy for what she goes through. Molly shows me how she can fight through her challenges and how I can fight through mine, which are so miniscule to what she deals with every day.

After running with the cross-country team and competing in the State Championship Race, I was battling a knee injury, which made it difficult to keep up with the hard training. This year, my doctor told me if I ever wanted to run again, I would have to quit the team and allow my knee to heal over a long period of time.

At first I felt the harsh reality of quitting a team that I put so much of my time and passion in, and also that my goal of running in college ending. I was devastated and hopeless for a couple weeks.

Then I remembered Molly, and how she faces the challenge of movement every day, and how it's a struggle just to hold up her head or communicate a single thought. And how that she didn't stop her from trying and being happy. The girl that needed my help with her challenges had helped me with mine. Now it's my turn to tap the saddle and "walk on" with my life.

ANALYSIS: This was a tough essay to write. Hannah walked a fine line when comparing the challenges of autistic kids to a knee injury she suffered. It's hard to make this comparison sound authentic, and not come across as an out-of-touch teenager.

But I think she pulled it off. She related the challenge of helping one specific student—Molly—and helped us see for ourselves the frustration and how even the most minor advancement felt like huge accomplishment.

When Hannah described her own personal injury, she helped the reader understand how this was huge obstacle for her, but also kept it in perspective. She went on to explain how she tapped similar qualities to deal with both issues.

This essay was all about how Hannah learned to keep challenges in perspective. And I think she not only learned how to do this, but helped us understand how she did it in her essay. This was hard to pull off. The best quality she revealed about herself was empathy, and that is a powerful equalizer.

Mitchell Wills
Laguna Beach, CA
University of Montana, Missoula, MT

The Grill Master

The smoke is almost blinding. Grease is spattering my face. It's a hot summer night, and the HOT grill is almost topping out at 500 degrees. As sweat starts to trickle down my back, I can hear my ravenous friends starting to complain. I slather another coat of marinade on the steaks, flip the chicken wings and roll the hot dogs a notch.

Some people would do almost anything to avoid the sweaty heat of the grill and pressure to produce a savory meal for their friends and family. Not me. Ever since 8th grade and I could safely operate a large gas grill, I've been the one responsible for the meat. Whether it's a barbeque at the beach or a sit down meal for a dozen good friends, I'm the one standing to the side, out of reach of the conversations and appetizers, carefully tending the mixed grill. I never forget an order. Medium rare. Well done. Cut in half. I make sure my food is cooked to order.

I am the Grill Master.

To me, barbeque is one percent inspiration and ninety nine percent perspiration and is not for the weak of heart. It takes a cool and passionate griller to make succulent, oozing, rich, mouthwatering, food every time they step foot near a grill. I will keep my Grill master title and work towards the even more challenging title of "King of the Grill".

Some people might underestimate the skill it takes to cook a slab of beef to perfection. The biggest threat to a perfect piece of barbeque is the flame. It's one thing to control the overall heat, but if you are like me, and don't take your eyes off the food for a second, you rarely burn the food. But sometimes, when the grease drips onto the flames, and they flare up engulfing the meat, you have to act fast. Fast as a cow on fire, I pinch it with the tongs and pull it off until the flames die down. Or, if I see it coming, I simply turn down the heat or shut the hood. It's all in the timing and constant attention.

The timeless phrase, "Strike while it's hot," can have multiple meanings with different interpretations. For me, it is the understanding that you put meat on the grill when it is hot to get the correct heavenly sound of the cold raw meat hitting the hot grill with an exquisite sizzling noise. Some people have said my barbeque "is so good it makes them want to return something they didn't even steal."

I notice that I save this type of intensity for these special occasions, when I'm feeding the people I love. Nothing makes me feel better than loading up a large platter with delectable array of meats, and watching everyone's reaction and comments. It doesn't even bother me that all that hard work is gone within ten minutes, and all that's left is a big pile of bones.

No one else knows I have deemed myself the Grill Master. But that's okay. I take a secret pride in my culinary skills, and will always be the first to volunteer to be the guy tending the smoking hot grill.

ANALYSIS: What's funny to me about this essay is that in-person, Mitchell comes across as a very laid back guy. So it was brilliant that he wrote his essay about this secret talent that requires such intensity and passion.

By focusing his topic on this single theme—that he prides himself in manning the barbeque—Mitchell revealed many other qualities about himself. He showed us that he has an internal fire when it comes to what he loves doing, and the people he loves doing it for.

Even though he didn't write this piece to be funny, it shows his sense of humor and wit. It worked because Mitchell wrote it straight, and didn't try to make it comical. Even his bravado was endearing.

I'm not sure Mitchell ever would have dreamed about writing his college essay about grilling meat. But his college admissions consultant, Lynn Fair, knew him and his reputation, and told him, "You have to write about that!" As usual, she was spot on.

Anna Heitmann
Laguna Beach, CA
University of San Francisco, San Francisco, CA

City Girl

I'm not sure what my brother and I were fighting about, but I stormed off into the crowd outside an old cathedral in downtown Barcelona. My mother had already gone her own way to shop, but now I was separated from my brother and dad. At first, I was sure they were following me. But when I turned to check, all I saw was a blur of strangers.

I tried to suppress the panic welling up inside me, as I knew that keeping a level head in such a situation would be crucial. But I began to feel overwhelmed by the noise and press of the crowd around me; everyone was speaking Spanish, a language with which I was completely unfamiliar. I began to walk very carefully up and down the street where I last saw my family, searching the many faces that passed me. The summer day seemed to only grow hotter, and all I saw were strangers.

It took everything I had not to panic. No cell phone. No money. And the name of our hotel had never really sunk in. "I can't believe I'm lost," I thought to myself, trying to not to break into sobs. I couldn't accept that this glorious city, which I loved even before I arrived in Spain, could betray me like this.

Since childhood, I have always loved big cities. I imagine myself a part of their countless stories, animated by the hum and clatter of the streets and the color and variety of thousands of different people and pastimes. I long to explore new cities, to feel the thrill of never knowing what I'll find down the next street. In my mind, everything is possible in a metropolis.

When I visited big cities as a little girl, my family would ask me what I wanted to do. Hitching my little pink purse up on my shoulder, I would always respond, "I want to walk around town." I have been fortunate to visit major cities on four continents. My favorites were the ones that were most exotic to me because they were more challenging to fully discover. It is always a bit intimidating trying to figure out how to get around or how to buy something in a shop or restaurant.

As I've grown older, however, I've gained more confidence in my ability to overcome shyness around strangers and language differences to conquer a city, explore it inside and out, find its treasures, and claim my small part of it. It is always an adventure, especially as someone who grew up in a small beach town, and I love nothing more than a chance to test my independence, logic, and resourcefulness.

But while hopelessly lost in Barcelona that summer, I only felt helpless and vulnerable. I finally decided to wait on the steps of the cathedral, hoping that my family would think to look for me there.

After waiting for an hour, I heard my brother call my name. I was overwhelmed with relief, and I could tell they felt the same. I never told them how terrified I had been. Even though that was one of the most frightening experiences of my life, I still love nothing more than exploring an unfamiliar city.

In a strange way, I almost can't wait to embrace the marvels of another immensely complex and dynamic urban environment, to find my way, and my place, in a new city. I have learned enough to be smart and safe, and that the trick is to maintain a level head and stay calm and confidant. I also know that mastery depends on keen observation, genuine curiosity, growing empathy, and a willingness to be surprised or delighted. I may get lost for a short time now and then. But I know I will get re-oriented and back on track. I'm a city girl now.

ANALYSIS: Anna was one of those students convinced she had "nothing interesting" to write about herself. I don't recall her exact list of interests, but they fell into the categories of most typical high school students: things like soccer, dance or a popular philanthropic club.

She hadn't faced any unusual challenges or crises in her life, and she loved things like horses and dogs. We also couldn't flush out any unique idiosyncrasies.

Like many students in our privileged town, Anna had travelled quite a bit with her family. As a topic, travel can sometimes make a student appear entitled, which is not something you want to flaunt in your college app essay.

But in talking with Anna, we dug a little deeper. What had she learned through all her travels? Not just about the places she visited, but about herself. And out popped a topic: Anna learned how to navigate cities and over time realized that she was a city girl.

She picked a simple anecdote to start her essay to show a typical city experience: getting lost. This gave excitement and drama to her essay, which did a great job of taking a simple incident and using it to reveal what she was all about.

Alex Hunt
Laguna Beach, CA
Cal Polytechnic State University (SLO), San Luis
Obispo, CA

Two Moms

Sitting in my freshman Spanish class, I listened as the teacher turned the conversation to our families. He started asking each student about their parents, both their mother and father. I felt a familiar sense of dread and anxiety deep in my stomach. But I was ready for my turn.

"*Que hace tu padre?*" he asked me in Spanish, meaning "What does your father do?"

As calmly and directly as I could, I explained to him in Spanish that I did not have a father because I have two mothers. They are lesbians.

I then had to explain, in Spanish, how I came into existence. My teacher, who wasn't shy in expressing his opinion, then argued that one must have a father figure and claimed that surely I must have some sort of male role model in my life. I explained that I did not have a father figure in my life and that I didn't believe a father figure was necessary because I had lived my entire life without one.

This is how it begins. About once a month, I'll have to explain to someone that I have lesbian mothers. And my explanation only leads to other aggressive questions about my family. Usually their inquisitions feel like a personal attack; sometimes they really hurt.

Most of the time, however, I just field their questions and let it go. People are often surprised to hear that I live a normal life despite not having a dad. Because I have lived my entire life without a father, I feel that not having a father is completely ordinary. It is actually strange to me to think about what it would be like to have a dad.

While sometimes I am judged because of it, having lesbian parents has taught me how to stand up for my family and for what I believe. Having to routinely defend my family has also helped me clarify my beliefs and values; I have learned the importance of tolerance. Because of my experiences with my family, I know that people deserve to be treated equally regardless of any superficial differences.

When I explain my family, there is the occasional person who will not only give me a hard time about my lesbian parents, but argue with me against the merit of homosexuality. Often, this person will claim that homosexuality is a choice, or that my parents should not be able to be married because homosexual marriage goes against the Bible.

These arguments have impacted me. When people make these arguments against homosexuality, they state their beliefs that my parents are not worthy of marriage and that there is something wrong with them.

The implications are that there is also something wrong with me. Over time, I learned to deal with these attacks. I learned that the attackers were often ignorant of my life, so I trained myself to understand that they only made the attacks because they did not understand my family. They only attacked my family because they were ignorant. I began to feel tolerance and sympathy even towards those who did not accept my family.

The questions about my father do not come up very much anymore, but when they do, I'm prepared. My family and the attacks against them have strengthened the tolerance and sympathy I feel towards those whose lives I do not fully understand.

I have learned to accept that some people are bound to be ignorant of my family and in turn have begun to tolerate and understand those people who are uninformed of my lifestyle. Even in the face of judgment and criticism, I can now maintain my sympathy towards others. I'm ready for the next question.

ANALYSIS: Alex wrote about a highly personal issue in his life, and pulled it off like a pro. He chose a perfect example of what it felt like to be him in his introduction. Instead of just telling the reader how having two mothers as parents could be awkward and difficult at times, Alex showed us with a real-life anecdote.

As with the best anecdotes, this real-life example put us directly in Alex's shoes—or the hot seat in his high school Spanish class. By recreating the innocent question the teacher threw at him, and his answer and the annoying questions that followed, the reader could get a sense of what it's like to be Alex. And we also saw how he handled these questions, and himself in general—using his wit, wisdom, tolerance and empathy.

What a winning list of qualities Alex revealed in this essay. He not only walked us through how he developed them over time, but also shared what he learned from them—he became a bigger person. I also love his ending, since he shows the reader how he will apply what he learned in his future: He's ready to face anything.

Paige Greenwood
Laguna Beach, CA
University of San Francisco, CA

Hip Hip Hurrah!

A disease plagues every member of my family: Greenwood hips. Scrolling through my father's vast collection of pictures ranging from baby photos to recent family vacations, I realized I had developed this dominant gene. I stared closely at a photo of my uncle, my father, my brother and I lined up on the shores of Hawaii and found that the wide hips on my torso mirrored those of my other family members. I was shocked.

It was a gene I had prayed to escape, and realizing that the abnormally wide hips had reached me crushed my confidence. I began exercising more, opening my schedule for daily hikes and weight lifting worthy of an Olympic athlete. I soon realized that no number on the scale could disguise the bulk I carried above my jeans. Even my brother who weighed one hundred pounds at the time and resembled a string bean wasn't able to escape.

Gathering with the rest of my diseased family on Sunday night dinners or family reunions, joking remarks would fly across the table concerning the unique body type that affected nearly all of the participating insulters. I couldn't understand how a family with such a terrifying gene disruption could express such obvious confidence. Watching my loud and colorful family proved to me that my confidence didn't have to come directly from my appearance. I grew proud of my hips, knowing it was a characteristic that made me a part of my family. At least I knew I wasn't adopted!

My confidence didn't only grow in my appearance, but my personality and my ability to be a leader. I realized that I was worthy of making decisions and found myself good at it. I raised my hand more often in class, declaring thoughtful remarks that would have otherwise gone unspoken. I had to take what I was given in life, and use it as tool. I discovered the power of laughing at myself. Gaining confidence from aspects outside of my physical appearance allowed me to raise my voice and find my true talents.

ANALYSIS: I remember when Paige read this essay out loud at one of my essay workshops with Lynn Fair. It was so delightful and perfectly illustrated the idea that you can write a great essay on almost any topic.

I liked how she kept it simple and her message direct. It's a powerful theme, self-acceptance, and I've read other essays that express it, including topics such as frizzy hair, freckles and weight issues. By writing about wide hips, Paige added an unexpected spin to this theme—who would have thought wide hips would be a problem?

She wrote about it in such fresh, matter-of-fact language. I believed this style in itself gave us a sense of Paige, in that she's a logical, no-nonsense kind of girl with a deadpan sense of humor. That she confessed that her hips made her self-conscious only makes her more accessible and likable.

At the time she wrote this, Paige said she was interested in becoming a nurse. To me, the qualities she revealed in this essay are exactly what I would want in someone taking care of me.

Margarita Fedorova
Moscow, Russia
As of publication, deciding between Carnegie Mellon University, Pittsburgh, PA, and the University of California, Berkeley, CA.

Cheesecake

First, melt five tablespoons of butter. Then add two cups of crackers to make the crust. Press into a spring pan.

"What the heck is a spring pan?" I thought, looking around my mom's kitchen

I read on. Two pounds of cream cheese. "Really, two whole pounds?"

A pinch of salt. "Salt in sweet cake? Hmm."

One and a half cups sugar. Four large eggs.

"Now, if I only knew how to break an egg…" I thought, feeling embarrassed by my own thoughts.

It's 2 am, and I am trying to make a cheesecake. It is my best friend's sweet sixteen, and I was foolish enough to promise her a culinary surprise. I was also foolish enough to think that there was nothing more to a cheesecake than putting cream cheese in a mold. For the past two hours, I have been learning I was wrong— the hard way.

Imagine a bad cook. Then, put a pot on her head. This would be me. When other girls learned culinary magic from their mothers, mine would call it "ungrateful labor" and tell me to do my homework instead. As a result, it's easier for me to solve a logarithm than boil an egg.

It's 3 a.m., and I just used a mixer for the first time. Judging from the shiny layer of batter on the cabinets, I suspect I did something wrong. Should I get her something else? What if I just buy a gift?

No, I promised. I am not backing down now. I'm in too deep. Crackers are broken and mixed with butter. It's time for the filling.

It's 4 a.m., and I am searching Google on "how to use a stove." If there's one thing about me, I'm stubborn. Maybe determined sounds better. But I would rather fail—even fail miserably, repeatedly, even publically—than give up.

My mind is burning. Don't forget a pinch of salt. Is this pan big enough? Where did I just put the foil?

It's 5 a.m., and OUCH! My fingers! Fifteen minutes and two Scooby-Doo Band-Aids later, I am back on track. Now I know not to check the stove's temperature by touching its insides with bare hands. I pour the filling into the mold, cross my fingers for luck, and put it in the stove.

It's 6 a.m., and starting to get light. It feels like I've finished a 10-mile run. I wipe sweat off my forehead and watch the insides of the pan turn light brown. Thirty more minutes. I was scared I would fall asleep and miss the alarm. "Remember how you went to snowboard practices at 5 a.m.? It's the same."

It's 7 a.m., and I think I'm done. I pull out the tray and take a close look at my culinary chef-d'oeuvre: slightly burned, with the left side sagging. I can't resist and scrape a tiny piece off the side: Hmmm, better than it looks!

Three years later, I have made seventeen more cheesecakes. Each one of them was better than the one before. Not to boast, but I've earned myself a little reputation among my friends as a whiz in the kitchen. No one needs to know I only have one specialty so far.

Like my other endeavors, anything from attempting a snowboarding feat to sticking out my AP Biology class even though the teacher showed endless PowerPoints, I refused to stop what I started until I reached perfection. And I don't care how many flops it takes to get there. Am I stubborn? Well, let's just say I'm determined.

ANALYSIS: I think Margarita's essay is delightful. She came up with the creative format—hanging the five-hour chronology of her cake endeavor by giving hourly updates—all on her own. The best narratives put the reader in the writer's shoes, and this one gets us as close as possible.

We understand her raw determination because she helped us feel her frustration first. The reader can almost picture Margarita with a "pot over her head," and feel her burned finger, and even taste the satisfaction when her lopsided cheesecake turned out delicious.

I am so amazed by students like Margarita who write their essays in a second language other than their native one. Notice how well she uses the English language, including snippets of dialogue, concrete details (the Scooby Doo Band-Aid), simple analogies, quoting herself and asking questions out loud, and throwing in bits of humor and self-deprecation.

She nails the tone—playful and funny, as though she is talking to you—yet packed with gritty stubbornness. What college wouldn't want someone as determined and delightful as Margarita?

Emma Barker
Laguna Beach, CA
Savannah College of Art and Design, Savannah, GA

Bessie

Last year my parents decided that it was time for our family to finally take our steps from communal living to compact communal living: An RV trip. Yes, after long months of studying that school year and dreaming of a tropical island with fruit drinks and sunsets, I was given a thirty-foot mammoth. My family and I refer to her as Bessie.

At first sight, my stomach turned and my dream of a relaxing vacation was shattered by the rented eyesore that lay resting in our driveway. I told my parents I wouldn't like the three-week trip; I assured them it would be miserable, that four people and a dog would never survive a road trip in a confined metal box rolling down Route 66 in one hundred and fifteen degrees and counting. I knew it, but the rest of my family refused to believe it.

Bessie carried us from national park to national park. I witnessed the vastness of the Grand Canyon, and many more mountainous earth structures. Although each night we retired to our run down rust bucket, Bessie became a comfortable home.

And although her tire blew out on a highway and her air conditioning died out when the thick heat filled every crevice of her being and stopped the stream of cool air from spewing out of her underbelly, she brought my family closer together. I realized that with every 5-mile climb came an incredible view. With every mile of high winds and dangerous thunderstorms Bessie plowed through, brought us to another one of earth's mysterious art forms.

As my family and I continued on our journey, Bessie's size didn't seem to matter to us. Through Bessie's windows, we all witnessed the beautiful land of the west. Lines continued in all directions. Every night, the sun and the horizon intertwined in a sea of warmth, slowly descending behind the mountains.

Every night we sat near the campfire beside Bessie, admiring the view, and sharing stories of our lives before our trip. I watched the smoke float and swirl in the dim light of the dying fire. I noticed the sound of silence, a peaceful hum that echoed throughout the stretch of flat lands until it met the rigid mountains, crawling up the sides until it reached the stars.

We almost forgot how crisp the brightness of stars diffused among the blackened sky. We stared up at them drinking hot chocolate, soaking up the stillness until our bodies were one with the land and the land was one with us.

To be completely honest, whenever I talk about my family's RV trip I only bring up the tire exploding or the bickering my family that I couldn't escape from. I've never realized how wonderful the experience was, and how glad I was to have trusted Bessie with almost a month of my summer.

Bessie did well, and my view on my life changed. Taking time to admire things we have makes life more meaningful. Taking time to admire the beauty of the West opened my mind to a larger idea.

Don't let life pass you buy, and don't waste life always waiting for the future. I was obsessed with school, college and success. My dream vacation was escaping all of that on a beach with white sand and clear water. Well, I realized life isn't about running away from my problems or fears. My family RV trip left me thinking about my life in the present.

Bessie and the experience I had with my family freed the part of me that only saw potential in the future. Nature's constant beauty reminded me that everyday I have a chance to enjoy life, I have a chance to love my family, and I have a chance to live my life right now.

ANALYSIS: *Emma's entertaining essay started with a problem: The last thing she wanted to do was travel in tight quarters with her family for nearly a month. After amusing us with the downsides of RV life, she revealed how she handled this unwelcome adventure—and then went on to reflect on what she learned.*

This formula worked perfectly, especially because Emma shared her funny sense of humor, using words like "rust bucket" and stories, such as the blown tire. Despite her initial negative attitude, we saw how she is the type of person to make the best of things. What an attractive quality to show a college!

Not only did Emma adjust to her trip, she realized some profound ideas, such as the importance of living in the now. So besides being witty, flexible and positive, Emma also naturally revealed herself as an insightful teenager, and someone eager to learn new lessons—even if they involved some extended discomfort.

Chase Williams
Laguna Beach, CA
Haverford College, Haverford, PA

Having the Last Laugh

Clicking through the television channels with a bunch of friends, I lingered on an old episode of *SpongeBob*. At first one of the guys objected, but the others gave silent approval. Even though no one wanted to admit it, we all wanted to watch our old annoyingly yellow friend. As we sat laughing at the silly, familiar jokes, I realized that this show had taught me a lot about life.

Ever since I was young, I have been obsessed with television, despite my parents attempting to curb me from the "brain melting" machine. As a 4-year-old, I would scale the TV cabinet to put the Barney video into the VHS player.

My parents should have known there was no keeping me from it. However, it wasn't until that night I re-watched *SpongeBob* that I realized all of this tube-time actually benefitted me.

The shows taught me serious lessons about the world and its nuances. That particular episode helped teach me about swearing. The writers' cleverness allowed them to deliver this life lesson in a way that made me think about it, but somehow still enjoy and laugh. And now I realize that as I grow up, I never really stopped watching these shows, they just got older with me.

At first, it was *The Simpsons*, a little more crude and mature than *SpongeBob*, but somehow had the same effect. The lessons learned were more mature, particularly the lesson I learned on vegetarianism. In this particular episode, Lisa declared herself a vegetarian after visiting the zoo. This episode exposed me to the social implications of choosing such a lifestyle.

I then progressed to shows like *South Park*, even more crude, raunchy, and controversial than the *Simpsons*. One particular example is the episode the "Book of Mormon." The writers portrayed the supposed ridiculousness of Mormonism, but in the end they twisted it showing the Mormons as the happiest people.

The writers of course wrote the episode brilliantly and hilariously, but at the end it really got me to think, "Am I wrong for judging people?" "Is it a bad thing if people want to believe things that don't make sense if that makes them happy?"

Today, I still watch new episodes of *South Park*, but my day-to-day viewing is more in the vein of Stephen Colbert, or Jon Stewart. They are able to cleverly convey political opinions and lessons much the same way as the cartoons. They are provocative and really get me thinking about the issues, even while I'm laughing.

So while some may claim the TV to be the "brain-melter," I see it as one of my greatest teachers. Through watching episodes, from *SpongeBob* to *South Park*, I have learned valuable lessons about respect, alternative lifestyles, and even religious conflict. My goal is to keep learning about life and values the best way I know how—laughing.

ANALYSIS: At first, Chase wasn't confident that writing about cartoons would make a great essay. It seemed too silly for a college application. But once he started thinking about what he learned from those shows, he realized they were more than just mindless animated characters.

This is just another example that any topic can lead to a meaningful essay. In this case, the topic had an unexpected twist, in that Chase made the case that his cartoon watching actually taught him some tough life lessons.

He also revealed himself maturing with the themes as the shows tackled more controversial themes as he got older.

My favorite part of Chase's essay is how he started by showing how he and his "grown-up" teenage buddies all silently wanted to watch one of their old favorite cartoon characters. It was a shared, unspoken desire to re-visit an old friend. That's a feeling we all can relate with and a perfect way to connect with your reader.

Clara Ross
Seattle, Washington
University of Washington, Seattle, WA

Time to Move On

As I ran past the one-mile mark, I felt a little woozy, but I might have been just tired. I stopped briefly to measure my blood sugar. While other runners glanced questioningly in my direction, I poked myself with the lancet, squeezed my finger, and collected a tiny droplet of blood.

Five seconds later, my blood sugar level flashed at 43—uncomfortably close to a level where I could pass out or have a seizure. Disappointed, I stepped off the racecourse and drank a juice box, waiting for my blood sugar to recover. This was the third race where I was forced to the sidelines.

I found out I was a type I diabetic at age ten, but after a few days spent in the hospital learning how to manage the disease, I returned to my life. However, everything had changed. Being a diabetic since 2003 has forced me out of many activities, but at the same time it has pushed me to be independent, to value my health, and, most importantly, to keep trying in the face of obstacles.

Every day, several times a day, I count my carbohydrates, inject my insulin, and measure my blood sugar. I've done this ever since my diagnosis. How many grams of carbohydrate in a slice of bread? About fifteen. In a can of coke? Around thirty-eight.

I have to know the exact amounts of sugars in everything I eat in order to dose my insulin correctly. Along with the food, I take my exercise, my emotions, and even the time of day into account. I'll get low blood sugar when I exercise, stress can raise my levels, and I tend to go low in the evening.

I remember the first time I gave myself my own insulin injection. Only a few months after being diagnosed, I woke up hungry, but unable to eat until I received my dose of insulin. Normally my mom would have done it, but she had gone for a walk with my dad. However, I wanted *breakfast*.

I gathered my courage and did what I hadn't been able to do before: stuck in the syringe. A few minutes later, I smiled to myself with pleasure as I ate my cereal. At that moment, I knew I could get through anything.

The one thing I never imagine it would prepare me for, however, was suddenly facing life alone. In 2008, during my freshman year of high school, both of my parents passed away from cancer and I moved to Southern California to live with my aunt and uncle. Although I still struggle with this loss, I know the lessons I have learned from handling a chronic illness will help me face my current challenges.

Diabetes hinders me in many situations, such as cross-country races, but it never stops me. While I could let the loss of my parents slow me down, I refuse to lose the vivacity for life they instilled in me. In order to accomplish this, I use the independence and self-awareness I've gained from my diabetes to have the freedom to live happily.

As I stood on the sidelines during that recent cross-country race, waiting for my sugars to slowly rise to normal levels, I reflected upon my recent losses. It was time to move on, I thought. I rechecked my blood sugar and saw that I had reached a safe level to continue exercising. By this time, all the other runners had passed me. I didn't win, but I fulfilled my own personal goal: finishing the race.

ANALYSIS: There are several essays in this collection where students write about losing loved ones. Often, it's only natural to start with the impact of that loss or tragedy, and go from there. That way, the reader can see and feel how it affected you, and then understand what you learned from it.

But Clara took another approach. If anyone wanted to start with a sensational tragedy, she certainly could have. Instead, she focused on another challenge, her diabetes, to show how she proved to herself how she could be strong and independent, and ultimately able to cope with the unfair, tragic loss of both her parents while she was in high school.

There was not even a trace of self-pity in this essay. Clara only briefly mentioned the loss in order to explain how part of her drive and motivation to excel was inspired by their examples. The obstacles in her path only made her stronger. And she did a masterful job of revealing her calm, measured and patient determination to keep moving forward.

To me, this essay was a great example of how when you have a sensational topic that the best way to write about it is in an understated fashion. Keep the tragedy in the background—the larger the hit, the easier it is for the reader to "get it,"—and focus most of what you have to say on how you handled it, what you learned from it and how it changed you.

Connor McCombs
Laguna Beach, CA
University of San Francisco, San Francisco, CA

Writer's Block

The scratching of a pen on paper. A pause followed by a sigh. A loud scratch as something was crossed out. Breathing slowly, I regained my thoughts and began the line again.

"Ezreal climbed out of the water and onto the small ledge where he..." no. Not right. Another scratch as I once again crossed out the words. I just couldn't get the right feel. I wanted him to be desperate, not just climbing casually out of the water, but when I tried for desperate it came across angry and crazed.

I heard my mom call me for dinner. Sighing, I closed the moleskin notebook and tossed it aside. I'd been in the stupor for almost a week. Every time I'd pick up my notebook, I just couldn't quite get it right. Nothing. It was really starting to worry me.

Of course I'd encountered writers block before. Everyone does. Who hasn't been holding a pen and staring at the same word for twenty minutes before realizing they'd been thinking of the epic ending to come instead of the problem the character currently faced.

But this was different. It wasn't like my brain didn't want to think about this moment, it was like the book itself had rebelled. Normally I'd just put it down and come back later, but my writing has always been where I feel safe. It's where my emotions aren't mine, so I'm not scared to show them. I have an infinite amount of faces each with a different outlook on life, and none of these masks are as weak as me. When you live in a world of paper with laws of ink, anything is possible.

In these books, I've summoned demons only to have myself appear as a glorious hero and vanquish them back to hell. I've been cast as the writer, director, producer, and actors of a never-ending drama. I am the jock, nerd, cheerleader, geek, teacher, and nobody all at once. And never have I been scared to enter this world and create. But now, the world had turned against me.

I no longer controlled the world. I couldn't even get in. I sit in a chair with a notebook and imagine the world that once protected me from the real demons in my life. The world that took me in when teachers put enough stress on me that I probably should have been institutionalized. The world that was there when no one else was. The world that never questioned me, only listened to my words and made them into something more beautiful than I could ever imagine.

But my mom was calling me to dinner. That world wasn't real, and if it was it wasn't in an inviting mood.

My mom didn't sound too inviting either. She yelled from the other room saying that my food was in the refrigerator and I could get it later.

Sighing, I looked at my notebook, a world that I felt at home in when the real world turned hostile. Why should I walk away because it wasn't as easy as it used to be? Nothing is always easy. I knew that, but knowing something and putting it in to practice are two very different things.

I took up the notebook once more along with my favorite blue pen (an important tool for every writer). Flipping to a new page I watched my hand move and ink flow like blue blood from the silver knifepoint. Of course I came back to the other one later, but this idea couldn't wait. I had the main characters already, and the plot, well, I'd plan that out later. I just had to get it down on paper.

ANALYSIS: When a student says he or she wants to be a writer, they automatically hold themselves to a higher standard when it comes to these essays. And Connor clearly rose to the occasion.

His essay featured all sorts of creative writing techniques—varying his sentence lengths and using phrases for effect; including snippets of dialogue to give it a narrative flavor, and a wonderfully earnest, humble voice.

Connor shared his deepest fear—not being able to express himself and his stories. The dreaded writer's block. I loved that he didn't even try to convince the reader that he got past it. We just know he will—based on how much his writing world means to him and his raw determination to find a way back into it.

Meriel Caressa
Seattle, WA
Accepted to many great schools, but as of publication,
leaning towards University of California at Los Angeles.

Something to Smile About

Although I was sitting in the far back of the classroom, I was mortified when my phone started ringing. I had forgotten to leave it in my locker before class started and it was tucked in my pocket instead. The teacher walked towards me after the third ring and stuck our her hand, demanding I turn it over.

"Why are you smiling," she asked me, as I fished out my cell phone. Even though she was in the middle of reprimanding me, I couldn't keep the corners of my mouth down. I was feeling embarrassed and upset, but I looked as though I was happy that she caught me. My broad smile only made her angrier.

My friends and my family tell me I smile all the time, and sometimes a little too much; so much that it scares them at times. I never realize that I'm smiling, but it's something that seems out of my control. In general, I believe it's because I'm happy and friendly. Yes, it has gotten me in trouble a few times, but it has also helped open many doors and forge relationships with people I otherwise never would have met.

Many people say that my smile lights up a room. I like to believe that creating a positive energy makes me more approachable and people would come up to me and say, "Well, you look happy," and just by that exchange we would start a conversation. Everyday, no matter if I am having a good or bad day, I would unconsciously think of moments in my life that have made me happy and I cannot help but smile about it. I believe a smile is contagious; it spreads like the flu. But it only spreads wellness.

My friends sometimes tell me that it scares them that I smile at nothing, but they would then smile or laugh as well, and when I ask them why they are smiling and laughing, they would say " I don't know, I'm laughing and smiling because you are smiling all the time."

I still catch myself smiling at the wrong time now and then, although it has been a few years since I actually got in trouble. If I feel nervous, anxious, or even upset, I still can't help breaking into a cheery grin. I would like to think that a smile, even when it's ill timed or even inappropriate, is better than a frown or angry expression.

A smile makes people's day a little brighter, even strangers. In life, it seems like the world reflects back what you put out in the world. Smiling has definitely created and improved relationships of mine, and I wish to always make everyone's day a little brighter somehow and continue to let my smile illuminate my bright future.

ANALYSIS: This is another example of what I call a "lighter" essay. On face value, the entire piece is only about one trait—that Meriel smiles a lot. How could a topic that seemingly superficial make a compelling college essay?

First off, this lightness is true to who Meriel is, and the upbeat vibe she sends out to the world. I saw this for myself. And it's a beautiful quality, which like she explained, also generates positive energy from those around her.

Meriel naturally revealed her ability to examine herself when she analyzed why she smiles all the time, and the good and bad of this habit. This is what gave depth to this upbeat essay—and most likely left the reader smiling.

Maya Keces
Laguna Beach, CA
University of San Francisco, San Francisco, CA

Just Play

As I set up my electric keyboard in a corner of the hotel bar, I assessed the older crowd of tourists and locals. Most were engaged in loud conversations, and didn't seem to notice that I was about to sing. When my fingers hit the first notes, they seemed to quiet down, but the chatting and clinking of drinks continued.

"Just play," I told myself, trying to ignore the clenching pain in my stomach.

I rushed through my first song, and didn't think the audience would even notice it had ended. To my surprise, most of them looked up and started clapping. As I continued with my set, I felt more at ease and by the end of the night standing in front of that boisterous audience felt both familiar and exhilarating.

That evening I realized that no matter where I played my music and sang, whether it was in the middle of a mall or at a local coffee house, I went into what I can only describe as the zone. Initially, I thought the audience would not relate to my songs, just as they may have thought that a young girl was not suitable to sing at a bar. Yet, singing my compositions that expose my deepest feelings and observations allows me to connect to people of all ages and cultures. Being able to play in front of an audience like this, however, took me years to work up to.

I first started experimenting on the piano when I found an old, dusty keyboard in my sister's room when I was about 13. I taught myself to play by ear, and then started writing my own songs. One day, my mom walked past the room while I was playing and stopped and said, "Is that the radio?"

81

I soon learned that my mom wasn't the only one who enjoyed my music. I became compelled to share my music so I started playing live at coffee shops and weekly at the local mall.

Last year, I was offered my first paying "gig" at an upscale hotel in my town. I was nervous because the audience would be mainly tourists with high expectations, and the manager who hired me would be watching closely. Standing up there was one of the hardest things I've ever done, but after the first couple minutes, I felt like it was where I belonged.

Music has changed me, maybe to the point that I neglect other important aspects of my life. When finals came around and I needed to crack down on my studies, I channeled my stress into writing music. When homework overloads became too much, I wrote music. Even when my friends wanted to hangout on the weekends, I would stay home and play the piano. Music eases my worries and allows me to further understand my own raw feelings.

My biggest fear is that my music doesn't bring people as much joy as it does for me. The perfectionist in me is not ever completely satisfied with a performance. This allows me to push myself to further grow, but also hinders my ability to celebrate all my accomplishments. I can't help it sometimes. As happy as it makes me, I get serious about music.

Now when I perform, I still gaze over the crowd and feel that familiar tingle of nerves. However, once the music starts, I easily ignore the hum of the crowd, and sink into the melody and lyrics. Whether I'm writing music or sharing it with others, I'm where I belong. I also now know how to carry that gentle confidence into the world, and am always looking for the next chance to share my joy.

ANALYSIS: What struck me about Maya's essay was that she showed a unique quality about herself. Unlike many essays where students like to showcase their "best sides," such as being focused, or determined or creative, Maya showed herself as vulnerable.

If you think about it, it takes a lot of courage to do that—both on stage in front of an audience of strangers, and in an essay like this. To me, it means that deep down you actually are quite strong and grounded.

Maya not only put us in her shoes during that intimidating performance at a bar filled with partying adults, but she also revealed her other insecurities around her passion of singing. She said her biggest fear was that her music didn't bring others the joy it brings her. Only a very generous, caring person has a fear like that.

Maya even used her essay to offer an explanation (not an excuse!) for some lower grades, which can often be an appropriate place to let colleges know why your GPA dipped at some point during high school. And she worked it in seamlessly, so you almost don't even notice.

Maya struck a highly personal note in this essay, and as a result, it sings as beautifully as she does.

Anonymous
Seattle, WA
Middlebury College, VT

Fearless

Where I come from being religious is unusual; Washington is considered the least religious state in the nation. Very few of my classmates go to church. The few who do probably would find my belief system rigorous and almost radical. Christian Science is most known for the practice of spiritual healing and for me, it is a way of life. It does not only come out in times of need, but is a part of my everyday existence and rids fear from each activity.

Being a religious teenager in a highly secular place can be difficult. Sometimes I have to admit I dread the cliché questions of friends: What do you do when you get sick? Why don't you go to the doctor? I can't believe you have never taken any medicine! But I patiently answer these questions and embrace this challenge because spiritual living is crucial to who I am.

For me, being religious doesn't just mean going to church every Sunday; it is a daily practice and supports a fearless approach to life. Although I may stand out in a crowd, and many of my peers don't understand my commitment to my religion, I don't compromise my faith. I have overcome countless scenarios with the help of prayer, including the biking accident I experienced while training for a 350-mile bike ride from New York City to Washington, DC.

Biking along Lake Washington, the trees flew past me and the wind whistled in my ears. The dry smell of summer filled the air, and my legs churned up and down. The wind was at my back, and I felt like I was flying. Seconds later, however, I veered out of control. My bike and I hit the pavement and skidded across the road.

After bandaging the scrapes and resting in bed, I actively prayed to be healed. Supported by my mom and a Christian Science Practitioner, my thought was transformed from fear of the accident to reassurance that I would be okay. My body certainly needed time to mend, but being freed from fear was the central benefit of this healing. I wasn't afraid to get back on my bike, and I trusted that my cross-country season and school attendance wouldn't be compromised by my accident.

Although my classmates and peers seemed surprised to see me active again, I knew that my quick recovery was because of my prayer. I rely on my relationship with God everyday, and not just to recover from accidents. For example, when presenting scientific research to an audience of Bahamian government officials last spring, I was fearful of stumbling through my speech. Turning to God, however, I found confidence and assurance that I could deliver my proposal with poise.

While summiting Mt. Baker in ninth grade, I prayed to know that the boundlessness of God would energize me on my ascent. My gratitude for the limitlessness that came from prayer enabled me to see what was possible. While I may be the only one praying for safety and freedom of fear in each of my endeavors, I feel the effect of prayer daily.

While I love to read all day long in the summertime, laugh hysterically with my friends into the wee hours of the night, and have dance parties with my family in the kitchen, my relationship with God is the most important aspect of my life. It has brought assurance that I can live free of fear. Although most people may not understand this and even think I'm a bit odd at times, I don't mind being different. I would never trade the freedom I receive from being a Christian Scientist in order to live a more secular life. I value both the peace and power this often-misunderstood religion brings to my life. The deeper I develop my spirituality and my ability to pray, the freer I am to be me.

ANALYSIS: Writing about religion used to be on my list of "Don'ts" for topics, along with politics and sports. But over the years, I have changed my tune. This student proved why and how you can write about a "sensitive" topic and have it work for you, not against you.

The key was how she didn't write about her religion, and only make the case why it was good for the world. Instead, she wrote what it meant to her life. There's a big difference. What's especially interesting about this religion is that it is not a mainstream belief system, which can make it more challenging to put into practice.

This student used this essay to reveal many sides of herself. Yes, she is religious and is defined by her beliefs, but she is also someone who has the courage and strong sense of self to be different from others.

She even used her unconventional religion to make the case that in everyday life she actually was quite "normal," and loved to laugh and be a typical teenager with her friends. This made her feel more approachable and balanced, as opposed to someone who was purely pious and dogmatic.

The writer proved again that it's not what you write about in your essay, but what you have to say about it. You can write about religion, or politics or sports, but you need to be careful that you make your main points about yourself and not just about these topics.

Cassidy Robinson
Laguna Beach, California
Hendrix College, Conway, AR

Outside the Lines

Sitting in my booster chair, I giggled and waved the green marker in the air when my mom walked into the room. I was about four years old, and had just discovered that I didn't need to stick to the flat piece of drawing paper. From my nose to my toes, my entire body was covered with green scribbles.

A lot of mothers might have groaned at the sight of my ink-covered body, and then launched into an angry lecture or even a spanking. Not my mom. She just looked surprised for a moment, then left to find the camera.

This was my earliest memory of how I got the idea that it was okay for me to express myself, even if it wasn't always a pretty picture. From that moment at the kitchen table through my elementary and high school years, my family has created a protected space for me to learn and explore my feelings and ideas. Not everyone, however, I met shared this value.

Some English teachers cared more about my spelling than my message; a few history teachers cared about my test results more than my interest in the current election; and sadly, most of my art teachers wanted me to reproduce what I saw instead of express how I felt about it.

But lucky for me, I always had someone pushing me to ask my own questions, explore my own priorities and create my personal style of expression. And it didn't matter if I made a little mess in the process. Ever since I was little, a box of crayons or a freshly made batch of flour-based Playdough has been within easy reach. Even at the beach, I was always dragging over the longest piece of kelp or the bulkiest chunk of driftwood to assemble into some type of bizarre beach sculpture.

Beside my mom's encouragement, my grandmother also fed my ideas about creative play and personal expression. Her name was Sally, but we called her Nana, the artist and potter who wore bold, ethnic prints and jangles and chunky jewelry. Whenever I stayed with Nana, she always had an art project ready. I remember when she had my brother and I turn large palm fronds into mask-like paintings.

It seemed magical how Nana used thick strokes of acrylic paint to create an exotic face on the rough wood. When I tried to paint my frond, the eyes of my face were lopsided and the nose did not look quite right. Eager to give up, I smeared the lines into a brown mess. Nana, however, told me, "Just turn it into something better." After it dried, I painted on another coat, then exaggerated the mistakes and incorporated swirls and fun organic shapes. It was still pretty ugly, but this time I liked it.

When I took art classes in elementary school, the teachers had us replicate famous art works such as Van Gogh's "Starry night" and Magritte's "The Listening Room." I enjoyed learning about these artists, but couldn't wait to get home and create my own crazy masterpieces. Middle school and high school were not much different. My junior high art teacher was very strict. Her goal was more about following directions than developing our own style.

Although I liked his enthusiastic personality, our high school art teacher stressed exacting still life studies and photographic replications. He thought a picture needed to be worked on for several weeks before it could be "good." Unlike my grandmother, he taught students to erase and start the piece over if was not coming together.

During all my classes, I always went with the program and learned helpful techniques and skills from my teachers. But I still follow my grandmother's advice of making mistakes into something better.

This advice has been helpful in my life as well. When I make mistakes I embellish on the fact and acknowledge my faults. I find beauty in nature's imperfections. I like people others avoid, and see that imperfections are often their best attributes. I know I have so much to learn from others, but I will always look to myself for my most creative and original work. Even if it's not picture perfect, I know that as long as I invest my heart and imagination in the process, it will be one of a kind. And so will I.

ANALYSIS: This was the first person I helped with a college application essay: My daughter! We started by brainstorming a real-life moment or "time" that would show the reader her creative side.

Cassidy described the "time" she drew all over herself, and how she was not scolded for that "creative" outburst, even though she was a mess. Then Cassidy recalled other times as she was growing up where she received the same lesson: That personal expression is more important than being perfect, neat or even obedient all the time.

By relating these experiences, Cassidy revealed her own independent spirit, and what she values the most in her life. In the process, she also helped us get a sense of her playful personality and bold sense of adventure.

Anthony Amato
Washington, CT
University of Michigan, Ann Arbor, MI

Modern Day Magic

Huddled around the dull, silver box, with a giant tangle of wires and cords behind it, we agreed it was time. Every bolt and screw was in place. I looked at my friend and nodded. With a quiet whir, our homemade computer came to life. Success! Hours of working in my basement finally paid off. But within seconds, it went dead.

The disappointment was gut wrenching. My two friends and I had spent hours building this contraption. And now it didn't work? "Wait," my friend said. "Did you plug the CPU to the motherboard?" Sure enough, it just needed power...

I've always been intrigued by technology. To me, it's modern day magic. I remember playing my Backyard Baseball games on my first desktop when I was 6 years old. I always had the latest Game Boy. When laptops hit the scene, I saved up for months to buy my first computer, an Apple MacBook, in 6th grade. As soon as Amazon released its Kindle Fire, it topped my Christmas wish list.

When my Apple computer finally broke, my friend recommended that I build my own computer. My first thought was, no way, I could never in a million years build a working computer! My second thought was that I thought building a computer meant soldering the wires together and creating my own case. I was wrong on both fronts. I learned that a DIY computer was possible, and that it was more like assembling a complicated puzzle.

Besides learning the complex steps required to build the equivalent of a mechanical brain, I also learned the value of details. My friends and I were 99.99 percent done with the project. We only needed one more component, but overlooking a small detail was critical. I couldn't believe I spent my time and money envisioning and building my dream computer for it to be a total flop. Thankfully, we only failed because we overlooked a small detail. But this got me thinking.

I remembered an argument I had with my dad over how my teacher graded my test. I lost all points on a question even though I almost had the answer. My dad said that my teacher did the right thing, while I felt like I deserved at least partial credit. My dad told me, "Imagine you're the crew that was responsible for sending men to the moon. If your team calculated the projection off by half a degree, those astronauts could miss their target."

No matter how hard you try or how close you come to mastering a project, one wrong calculation or missing detail can offset the whole project. I like to think of myself as a big thinker, someone who loves a complicated challenge. But I've also come to appreciate the value of precision, especially after seeing for myself what's at risk. One small detail might not seem important at the time, but in its greater context it could mean everything.

ANALYSIS: It can be challenging to write an interesting essay about things like science and technology. But Anthony made his passion for fixing and inventing come alive mainly by telling us little stories and offering specific examples.

He also injected feelings into the sometimes colorless world of gadgets and computers. His introduction shared the sense of defeat when their hand-built computer died, but then surprised us when he told us it was simply out of juice.

Sharing these types of emotions showed that even though Anthony was obviously a smart, logical guy, he also had a balance in his personality—something colleges love to see.

Carolyn Bai
San Diego, CA
Cal Poly San Luis Obispo (SLO), CA

Coming Full Circle

At the end of my first ice-skating competition, I concluded my performance with a basic two-footed spin. But as *The Little Mermaid*'s "Under the Sea" echoed across the ice, the audience began to swirl around me. I realized that the music was far from over. So I just kept spinning. And spinning.

Even though I was only six years old, I kept my blades moving and maintained my steely focus. I kept circling the ice, listening closely for the final notes. There was no way I was going to finish my performance before the music ended.

Ice-skating began taking over my life when I was just four years old. I would wake up before sunrise and practice two hours every morning before school. The ice rink became my second home. The five a.m. wake up call was the drive that kept me motivated.

The sport required the dedication to excel, the confidence to perform, and a strong mindset to conquer failure. Those metal blades may have been thin and overshadowed by the pure white skates, but they contained a line of stability; a sense of reassurance that ice skating would always keep me in balance, both mentally and physically.

After nine years of strictly devoting myself to two thin steel blades and buildings kept below freezing, I began to question the passion I thought would last a lifetime. Ice-skating defined who I was. It portrayed my natural grace and determination, while my unconditional devotion to the sport brought out my confidence. Thoughts of letting go of something I worked half of my life to achieve scared me. How could I possibly give up the one thing that fueled who I was? Who would I even be without ice-skating? If I let go of my life on the ice, where would I land?

Once I started high school, I forced myself to try new experiences, including field hockey and different volunteer and leadership activities. Being away from the ice made me feel unstable at first, but I was surprised to see that I was able to redirect my drive, focus and motivation from ice-skating. As I let go of the persona of my ice-skating world, I realized my strengths translated into new areas.

In my experience with TEDxYouth@SanDiego, an independently organized event created by fifty high school students, I transferred my skating confidence and energy into becoming a team leader. I was able to bring some of the world's most intellectual individuals to the stage of my own high school. The event, held for over 400 youth around my community, inspired individuals to take action upon their big ideas and work beyond boundaries to make their mark on the world. By chasing after these new opportunities, I discovered I had even more confidence off of the ice than on.

Every once in a while, I still miss the adrenaline rush from performing in front of hundreds of people. I will never forget that first competition where I spun and spun until nailing my performance on the final note of the song. But each new challenge I take on offers new goals to meet and qualities to develop and share. To this day, I am still making room for greater experiences and newfound passions, while learning to let go of others. No matter what I try next, I know that I will keep on spinning until the music stops.

ANALYSIS: I loved Carolyn's essay for several reasons. First, I liked how she used an anecdote to start her essay, and how she left it open-ended and picked up her mini-story at her conclusion. This gave her essay a pleasing sense of continuity—she came full circle, literally and figuratively.

When she relayed her real-life moment on the ice as a young skater, she didn't tell us exactly how it ended up and left us hanging—or spinning. This was a powerful device to engage readers and created suspense to make them want to read on.

Carolyn also did a nice job of using her skating story to highlight her qualities both on and off the ice—telling us why she let go of that passion and brought along qualities she learned there. She was able to naturally work in other interesting experiences, including the TED talk conference.

By sharing a life transition in this essay, Carolyn revealed several qualities about herself that she didn't even mention, such as courage, boldness and maturity. It's impossible to let go of self-defining activities to explore new horizons without these qualities. This is why when you share your stories. You naturally expose your true nature—and that's what you want with these essays!

Duncan Lynd
Laguna Beach, CA
California State University, Long Beach, CA

That Takes the Cake

When I woke up on my ninth birthday, I could barely contain my excitement. I knew that later that day my friends would soon join me to celebrate. We would smash a piñata, I would get to open presents, and we would all get to eat cake. Out of every fantastic thing about my birthday, the cake was my favorite. Every year, when my mom brought the cake out, my heart would skip a beat in excitement.

My mom always went above and beyond when she made a birthday cake, which would range from three feet to six feet, from the Pokémon Pikachu to, in this case, the Jedi Knight Yoda. I loved watching, and occasionally helping, her make the cakes, especially my role licking the spoon. The cakes that she made were one of the many things that intrigued me about baking.

My love for culinary creation, however, first started when I was 18 months old, when I would make things called, "Yummy Tummy Sandwiches." These "sandwiches" were essentially anything that I could get my hands on and enclose between two slices of almost anything else. My favorite sandwich: peanut butter, pickles, ketchup, and ham, all stuffed in between two sugar cookies.

I would always give these sandwiches to my parents, assuming they would eat them. Recently, when I asked my parents about them, I discovered that my mother never ate them, but my dad always did so as not to hurt my feelings. I loved making these sandwiches for my family; it was one of the building blocks that support my love for culinary art today.

Eventually, my sandwiches grew into legitimate food as I discovered that people like eating good foods that complement each other. My childhood culinary experiences peaked during a Thanksgiving about seven years ago. It was anarchy in my house because my mom was in the hospital undergoing emergency surgery, and we were all terribly worried about how healthy she would be afterwards.

When she came out of the surgery, the doctor told us she would be fine, but needed to rest for two weeks. We were ecstatic. When I realized that my mom would not be able to cook Thanksgiving for the family, I bought the subject up to my dad. He said, "Well, I guess it's your turn."

So, I got my dad's credit card and walked down to the store with a shopping list containing Thanksgiving essentials: turkey, stuffing, sweet potatoes and a few, not so typical ingredients. At dinnertime on Thanksgiving Day, I laid everything out on the table and told everybody that it was ready to eat. They were in awe. The expressions on their faces were priceless—they never thought that an 11-year-old child would be able to make a Thanksgiving feast.

Even though I have helped out every Thanksgiving since, I found my true love of the culinary arts in baking. I would bake cakes for everyone's birthday, Mother's day, Father's day, and even Saint Patrick's Day. One time, for my friends 16th birthday, I made him a cake of his dream home—which looked like a massive estate, with a volleyball field, a pond, and a castle in the middle.

The reason that I love to bake cakes for everyone is because of that feeling that I got when my mom made cakes for me. That feeling where you know that somebody loves you enough to sacrifice hours of her or his time, in order to make you happy. I enjoy making other people feel that way.

ANALYSIS: Yes, this is the same student who wrote about being the big guy who everyone thought was mean. This essay was equally good. Again, he chose a topic that showed an "unexpected" side of himself—he loved to bake. This was not a common passion among most teenage boys.

So from the start, we were interested to hear about this hobby, and enjoyed learning what sparked it. Notice the details Duncan shared in this essay that really made it come alive.

He didn't just tell us he loved to bake, he gave us colorful details: Who doesn't love the story about his "Yummy Tummy Sandwiches?" and that his dad pretended to eat the strange concoctions so not to hurt his feelings.

And there's an even more endearing element behind the baking—it's how Duncan shows his love for people in his life. That's a quality I believe would be hard for anyone to turn down—even colleges.

Cassidy Robinson
Laguna Beach
Hendrix College, Conway, AR

Standing Up

For the third time in an hour, the wind snapped my homemade sign out of my fingers. After chasing it down the sidewalk, I grabbed the placard again and lifted it high in the air. Rain pelted my face. "No toll roads through state parks!." I shouted along with the handful of other protesters.

Stuck in traffic along the main drag through our coastal city, most people watched sympathetically. They honked horns, shouted encouragement and gave appreciative nods. Others, however, were not as supportive. One man slowed his car next to me and waved an offensive hand-sign. Another stopped long enough to shout ugly words, then peeled away.

Standing in public, chanting slogans and waving signs in the rain wasn't my favorite way to spend a Saturday morning. But when it comes to the environment—in this case, the future of my favorite local state park and beach—I decided to spend my free time fighting to preserve open space and unspoiled beaches. Even if it means enduring verbal assaults from strangers, unpleasant circumstances or unpopular issues, I believe that defending nature is worth the time and effort.

I do not recall when my love of the environment began; maybe I was born with it. Even in the third grade I was trying to solve problems. My third grade invention measured six inches tall and balanced on three functioning wheels. The poster painted wooden base read "Oxygenated-Carbonated Car" on its side. Atop the green base sat a small flowery plant. The car ran off of the plant's oxygen; theoretically it did not pollute.

Visiting my grandmother's cabin in New Hampshire every summer also developed my passion for nature and the environment. Ever since I was a baby, my family spent a couple weeks in her rustic cottage on little Greg Lake. It was always a simple vacation, where we picked blueberries, canoed around beaver dams, and watched thunder storms roll in. But over the years, I have come to appreciate and love the natural beauty.

Along with our New Hampshire trips, our yearly family backpacks have shaped my appreciation for the environment. Last year, with my dad, mom and younger brother, we hiked up the John Muir Trail outside of Lone Pine.

As we left the wildflowers of the meadows behind, we watched how the dead tree trunks mimicked sculptures in their organic twists and turns. The connection in the elements created an indescribable beauty; one rarely captured in photographs.

Since we are lucky enough to live near the ocean, I grew up with a respect for the beach and coastline. Whether I was five or 15, we explored the local tide pools, built sandcastles out of driftwood and trash, and surfed the waves on boogie boards or surfboards.

I can trace my love of forests, mountains and the ocean to these activities. But now that I am older, I understand that they are all threatened by people who want to make money off them, and they need us to protect them.

During high school, I scoured our beaches picking up trash and awakened an hour on school days to scoop water from the ocean for water quality testing through sponsored by our local Surfrider Foundation and the Sierra Club.

About five years ago, I also learned about a larger, local fight to protect one of our most popular California state parks, called San Onofre State Beach. A local developer wants to build a massive toll road directly through this park, which would ruin some of our last remaining open space, public campgrounds, an ancient Native American burial ground, and destroy a wildly popular surf beach, called Trestles.

It was such an obvious travesty. So I jumped in to do what I could to fight this road. Along with my family and a few friends, we have worked to rally thousands to attend critical hearings regarding the future of this road, attended protests on street corners, distributed bumper stickers and fliers, recruited friends through Facebook, and I even had the opportunity to talk to delegates during the state Democratic convention last year.

The battle to save this park is ongoing. I'm starting to understand that when it comes to defending our natural resources, the fight may be never-ending and that we all must play our role as stewards of the ocean, mountains and forests. I realize that by banding together, we can make a difference. Even if it means standing in the rain on a street corner, I believe we must do whatever we can to protect what we love.

ANALYSIS: The thing Cassidy did in this essay was "show" the reader how she cared about the environment—even when it wasn't fun or pleasant—instead of just "telling" about it. How did she do this? Notice the first paragraph sets her right in the middle of a protest rally.

In this anecdote (or mini-story), which took up the first two paragraphs, she used sensory details to recreate the scene and helped us visualize what she went through. We could "see" the homemade sign, and "feel" the rain pelting her face, and "hear" the angry shouts from passersby. She also powered the scene by using active verbs, such as "snapped" and "grabbed," "honked," and "peeled" away.

Cassidy didn't just explain what she values—about nature, the environment and taking a stand for what she cares about—she "showed" us with examples. How she made a car in third grade that was supposed to clean polluted air. How she grew to appreciate nature during visits to New England and the local beaches. And how a threatened state park ignited a passion to save places that mattered.

Anyone who reads this essay can quickly get an idea of her "defining" qualities: Determination, passion, concern for others and the future, and a nature lover. All good stuff for future college students—and the world in general.

Chloe Mansour
Laguna Beach, CA
Boston College, Boston, MA

Family First

"Have you heard anything?" I asked my mom as I walked into her room, long past midnight.

"Nothing yet," my mom replied, wiping the tears from her eyes.

As I embraced her, I got the most horrible feeling in the pit of my stomach as a text appeared on her phone from my nana: "Honey, Dad passed away five minutes ago. He looks peaceful. I love you. Mom."

Words can't describe the complete state of despondency that swept over me at that moment. Suddenly nothing felt real. This wasn't happening. He wasn't really gone, not my grandpa – the most hardworking, generous, and humble man I have ever known; the rock of my entire family; my ultimate role model. Unfortunately, this was reality. After a 14-month battle with pancreatic cancer, my grandpa had lost.

The days following his passing were the hardest I've ever had to face. Everything that I did reminded me of my grandpa. Driving a car reminded me of when he taught me how to drive. Playing tennis reminded me of how he coached me to make the varsity team.

Working on college applications reminded me of how involved he had been in the whole process, even creating a notebook full of information on the colleges that he thought would be perfect for me. But more than anything else, my thoughts were filled with regret. All I could think about were the times I mindfully missed a family gathering for an outing with my friends or a head start on my homework. I wanted nothing more than to go back in time and put my family – my grandpa – first.

As my feelings of sorrow became more manageable with time, my outlook on life was forever changed. I thought back to previous times that I had been unhappy. I recalled the day I was upset over a fight with my best friend, the week I stressed over an English essay, and the night I cried because of a break-up. The thought of getting upset over these miniscule problems now seemed ridiculous to me.

Had these situations really been sources of grief in my life? Compared to dealing with the death of my grandpa, these troubles were unimportant. I felt ashamed that I had let those things bother me at a time when I was still fortunate enough to have my grandpa around. So I made a promise to myself to start putting everything into perspective and cherish what I have while it's still here.

Although I miss my grandpa more than ever, I find comfort in knowing that he is now in Heaven, completely out of pain. Losing him has taught me to truly value my family and all of the precious time that I have with them. They are an amazing blessing to me that cannot be taken for granted. I now make a concerted effort to put my family first, just as my grandpa did.

ANALYSIS: Writing about the death of a loved one often topped the list of college essay topics to avoid. The logic is that they have been written before and often don't reveal much about the writer. Instead, they risk sounding sentimental, nostalgic and cliché.

Chloe, however, showed us the impact of the loss of her grandfather by describing the moment she found out about it. Anyone who has lost a loved one couldn't help but feel her pain. It's a moment that not only engages readers, but connects them through shared experience and emotion. This is what you want in a narrative essay, but you must quickly move on to make sure the essay is about you, and not the person you lost.

That is the most important goal when writing your essay about someone else: You need to make sure most of your essay reveals your qualities, ideas, insights and goals. And not spend too much time on the drama of the crisis or the personality of the other person.

Chloe did a nice job of mixing in how her loss affected her emotionally, and how she handled those feelings. The most important part of her essay was when she explained her loss and feelings and reaction to them.

She talked about how they changed her, and how she found a fresh perspective on life and made new priorities. Chloe shared what her grandfather taught her, and what she learned from him even after he was gone.

Annabel Pascal
Laguna Beach, CA
Tulane University, New Orleans, LA

Crow

With my hands flat on the floor, and my elbows propped on my bent knees, I learned forward into the yoga pose. Wobbling from side to side, I struggled to keep my balance. My toes kept grazing the ground, when they should have been at least a few inches off the ground.

My fingertips trembled as they bore all my weight in this tricky balance move. Moments before my elbows caved, I felt a strong hand move each of my palms a tiny bit outward. The trembling stopped and my feet stopped kicking around. Finally, I found stability in my Crow Pose.

I had been taking yoga classes for the last couple years, but Crow Pose was something I could never master. Transferring all my weight towards my hands made me uncomfortable; therefore, I struggled and kicked around until the teacher called for us to change poses.

But this time, the teacher came to me and moved my hands. His simple gesture transformed my ability of holding the pose for a second or two, to about ten or eleven seconds.

I looked around the room and saw several other people struggling to maintain their pose. Even the times when I had collapsed on to the wooden floor, I had never heard a single giggle or felt a mean look from any of the other students. All I ever feel was their quiet supports. We were strangers, aging from thirteen to sixty-five, yet we all worked towards a common goal: peace of mind.

When my caving elbows straighten and feet stop kicking, I knew I had reached my peace of mind. Everyone's moment arrives at a different time, but with that moment, all other worries from the outside world dissolve. Problems with family, friends, and school cease to exist as I shift my focus from the overwhelming world around me, to discovering peace of mind.

Although my yoga studio is located just a few miles from my house, it offers a completely different world. Outside, people pressure me to succeed; here, people encourage me to succeed. Once I discovered yoga, I knew I would never be able to leave it. Every moment I could spare, I attended a yoga class. The peace of mind I achieved there was unlike any other experience.

Even though it often proved a struggle to reach my peace of mind, and I did not achieve it during every class, the process was worth the wait. It taught me discipline in an unexpected place, for I never imagined that yoga class would reap such a reward, let alone be difficult.

As I checked the class schedule to figure out a class that fit between school and homework, I realized that yoga class was not the only place I could attain peace of mind. Just as I struggle to work through a pose and reach my peace of mind, I find the same moment of happiness when I submit a paper after having difficulty to complete it or resolving a conflict between friends. Overall, my yoga class became my second home. Yoga taught me that through the stress and the struggles of life, peace of mind is always there.

With any obstacle that appears in my life, with focus and determination, I can overcome it. Every time I remind myself of this, my mind wanders back to the difficulty I had with crow pose. All it took was a bit more determination and a helping hand to reach my peace of mind in the pose. Any time I struggle, I reflect back on crow pose and remember that any struggle produces an even greater reward.

ANALYSIS: Annabel did a wonderful job of helping us "see" her struggling with a problem: a difficult yoga pose. She then went on to help us understand how she used this simple challenge to handle larger problems, such as stress.

I'm not sure she intended to do this, but Annabel used the Crow Pose as a metaphor for life challenges. This was a sophisticated writing technique to toss around deeper ideas.

It's funny that that was exactly what a yoga practice is supposed to do as well—use the lessons from mastering gymnastic-type moves to everyday life.

The beauty is you aren't even aware she is doing this, and all you enjoy is the simple story of her challenge, and what she came away with in facing it head on. Ultimately, Annabel revealed that she is someone who values balance in her life—even if it takes falling over every once in a while.

Emma Barker
Laguna Beach, CA
Savannah College of Art and Design, Savannah, GA

Soul Seeker

I had a heartbeat in every part of my body; I could hear the pounding in my ears and feel it in the tips of my toes. I reached the top of the stairwell to be met by a tall white-haired man. His bright red suit was hard to miss.

"Hello," he said, and gestured to the open door. I smiled, not out of courtesy but out of pure fear, not because I was walking into a stranger's apartment but because this stranger was a brilliant, professional Italian artist. We shook hands and I walked past his towering wooden door.

The online studio class in Italy depicted a friendly, walkabout art class that explored the city of Florence with perfect English speaking professors. Why do I trust the Internet? I realized that stupidity upon standing in front of a tall Italian apartment building, alone. My first thought, why did I come alone?

Although Florence is a large foreign city, seventy-five percent of it is red-faced, oversized, and perpetually lost tourists; not very threatening. Therefore my parents would rather grab an Italian coffee, than escort me to my art lesson. I didn't really know what I was getting myself into. Oh right, an art lesson from a guy who speaks zippo English, thanks Internet.

I walked into a heavy stream of light cascading down the opened windows. He sat me down, and without speaking, like I would understand him if he did, started drawing a face. When I tried to talk, he ordered me to watch, pointing at my eyes, then continued working. I listened. I watched. I interpreted.

"Now..." the artist struggled to spit out while handing me the pencil. He swiftly slides off the paint-splattered seat, raising his eyebrows, tracking my steady hand. I clenched the pencil. He waits for my first move, my first step to completing my task. My wrist rotates, floating the pencil over the paper. Pencil touches paper. He leaves with cigarettes in hand.

I still remember the way my mind melted away the sounds from the street windows, allowing the passage of rumbling motorcycles to fade into the scratching of my pencil. How lingering smoke drifted into the studio from the other room as my hand continued constructing the face with no name. My stomach twists but my eyes remain focused and determined. I am scared of rejection. I'm scared at the realization that my talent isn't good enough. This man, this studio, this city will tell me the truth.

The studio, although large and quite, appears intimate and very much alive. The artist's paintings clutter every corner; his expression fills the eyes of all the nameless people he has created. I've been told that looking into a person's eyes is like peering into a person's soul. As I worked, I wondered that if a painting or drawing has eyes, do they have souls? I realized that in order for a face to look real, it must have eyes that look as though the piece has a soul. Eyes that make people believe the painting is living, is breathing.

I hear the door to the apartment open. My hand freezes. My hand convulses as it constructs its final overview, making sure every angle, shading, and portion is correct. Now one would think that I would be missing the Internet's lies, it's fake walkabout tour, the flawless English, but at that moment I truly felt happy, scared out of my mind, but happy.

I was proud. I faced my fears and dug deeper into who I was as an artist. People aren't going to baby you through life. Life's about being alone, scared, and hopeless. It's about fighting your way through the hard parts and finding what kind of a person you really are. When my professor strolled in, cigarettes smoke clinging heavily to his loose clothes, his eyes reached over the table towards my work. I took a deep breath in, trying not to show him weakness by smiling and felt his eyes searching my work's eyes, looking at my newly fulfilled soul.

ANALYSIS: *This essay reads almost like a short story. You get a sense of the dramatic setting in Florence, Italy, by Emma's use of sensory details. The red-faced tourist; Italian coffee; and "light cascading down the open windows."*

Emma's artistic sensibility shined through in this essay. She noticed everything, and chose to share with us an experience that scared her to death. She never totally lost that fear, but embraced the excitement and potential of the unknown.

Through this piece, we got to know Emma, and how she feels and thinks about what she cares deeply about—making art.

Katie Hill
Whittier, CA
University of California at Berkeley, Berkeley, CA

Standing Tall

Standing with my back against the garage wall, I waited patiently as my dad placed the wooden ruler flat on top of my head.

"You have got to be kidding me," I thought to myself, as he began to read the numbers aloud. I had just started 7th grade, and I had already hit 5 feet, 10 inches.

It was a family ritual. Once a year, my dad pulled out the ruler passed down from his grandfather, and scratched my height on the wall. When I was little, I couldn't wait to see how many inches I had sprouted over the year. But this time, and every year since, I wasn't so eager to measure my height.

I have been back to that wall five times since that day and it is now covered with numbers, lines and smudges documenting my brother's and my growth over the years. Much to my chagrin, my current height mark is just shy of 6 feet, 2 inches.

By middle school, I was hard to ignore and very self-conscious. My height was a constant reminder that I was different, which was torture for a junior high school girl. Kids called me "bean pole" and "amazon." One kid even called me Chewbacca. Ouch, that one hurt. I tried to hide my height by purposely bending at the knees in our class picture so I would be placed with the "regular" sized girls, rather than in the back row with the boys. My trick worked, but my awkwardness persisted.

By the start of my freshman year, I found the classroom desks to be awkwardly sized and difficult to get in and out of.

111

My knees bruised from hitting the bottom of the desk when my legs were bent normally, but if I extended them, my size 11 feet inevitably smacked the person in front of me, prompting a look of reproach. My geometry teacher placed me in the back of the classroom, saying that I "was simply too tall to sit toward the front." My friends wore long, beautiful gowns with high heels. I wore short dresses and flats. I didn't begrudge my friends for this, but I ached to wear stilettos with a dress that dragged slightly on the floor.

People joked that I was "vertically challenged," but with high school came more confidence. I learned to embrace my over-sized, difficult-to-shop-for, towering self. Through highly scientific research (Google), I found a statistic that 99.996% of women were shorter than me. This Center for Disease Control study confirmed that I was in the rare group of only .004% of women in the United State that were 6 feet 2 inches or taller. How cool is that?!

I realize I am an oddity, but knowing that statistic makes me happy. It puts into perspective how rare, out of the ordinary and blessed I am. I can reach the last jar of creamy Jiffy Peanut Butter on the top shelf. I can always see over the crowd, something that came in very handy at the Hunter Hayes concert last August. I was even able to repeatedly make defensive blocks on goal in my CIF water polo championship game last season, a feat that shorter girls have no chance of performing.

Statistics have shown that taller people are perceived to be more intelligent, are instinctively turned to as leaders and have earned more money than shorter people. I'm eager to confirm that trend.

I'm different because of my height, and that alone makes me feel stronger. My life isn't just about being tall, it is about standing tall. I wear all 74 inches of my height with pride, gratitude and an elevated sense of justice. I've even started to wear heels, just to make people look twice.

ANALYSIS: *Kate wrote about being really tall. It was a natural topic for her, because it was defining. The challenge was to find unique things to say about it. And she did just that.*

Kate gave us very specific examples of what it meant to tower over her peers at a young age, and most importantly, put us in her shoes. We felt her awkwardness. She didn't make us feel sorry for her, just helped us understand the nuances of being big when everyone else was smaller.

"I ached to wear stilettos with a dress that dragged slightly on the floor," she said. Kate made herself vulnerable with statements like these, which endeared us to her plight.

Sharing your weak moments, times you feel sad or hurt, can be very universal. We have all felt that way, and it helps us connect with you. To me, this is what set Kate's essay apart—not just that she was tall, but that it gave her a unique perspective on life. And she really nailed it with her last line, a memorable, funny "kicker." Works every time.

Rian Atherton
Laguna Beach, CA
California Lutheran University, Thousand Oaks, CA

A Good Read

I was a god, omnipotent and all-knowing, my power remained undisputed, and the world lay there for me to shape in my image. Then SMACK!

"Stop reading your book, Rian," says my teacher; my only response to this was to pull out another book.

I will be the first person to admit I might have a little problem; I read way too much. When others hang out with friends, I read. When the teacher is speaking and lecturing, I read. Even if the world was ending and the four horsemen were riding across the sky, I would still be reading.

I think I have always used reading as an escape from everything. When I was a kid I would get teased for being fat or clumsy. Before I started reading, my response to this was to take the nearest object and strike whoever teased me. So I started looking at books and became a little bit obsessed. Reading provided an escape from my temper and from the dullness of life.

Through books I was set free. I was no longer limited by the world. I could be anyone, go anywhere, and nothing could ever hold me back again. I found that each book carried its own little world within it, and with them I could travel across the stars or dive into the deepest oceans. I became anyone I wanted, some evil villain with a master plan, or an archangel rising from the ashes caused by Lucifer's fall.

With books, I became a legion of stories and possibilities that was ever expanding. This helped and hindered me in the real world as well. I became more focused. Where once my attention strayed due to loud noises, I could now block out the distractions.

My temper, which was once out of control, had been reigned in and fettered so I no longer snapped and lashed out at every little thing. Finally my imagination was stronger than ever, for what was the most fun for me was putting myself in the books and acting out my own story instead of the one written down for me.

Unfortunately, my reading has also caused me problems. I have gotten into arguments with my teachers over books. One time in particular I started arguing with my teacher on how to properly treat books when she slapped my book instead of treating it gently. I have become more introverted and more nervous about talking to people and try to avoid it whenever possible.

One time I read all day nonstop I am not even totally sure what happened I read in class, read during break, read during lunch, read during practice, read while I was walking home, and even read during a team bonding session until my teammates took my main book and three backup books away from me.

Today my reading still poses a few problems. My teammates still are forced to steal away my books during bonding sessions, but I no longer read while the teacher lectures, which has cut down on book confiscations. Reading is still what everyone identifies me with.

If anybody wants to find me, they just look for the guy that reads a lot. Some might dislike this, but for me it sets me apart and I welcome it. So while yes reading has caused me a few problems, I still wouldn't give it up for the world.

ANALYSIS: Rian had the perfect problem for a college app essay: reading too much. It's a wonderful twist—how can anyone read too much? Even though it got him in trouble, he showed that he values learning and exploring life and ideas through books—and he's willing to risk it.

Now that's the type of attitude I would want from a student in my college. He's fierce about learning, takes it very seriously and even confides that he used books as an escape from other problems. This confessional quality only makes him more endearing, as someone who takes responsibility for his issues and seeks productive solutions, such as reading.

Rian also addressed a more universal question: Can you do something good, such as reading, too much? Even though he showed us many examples of times it seemed as though he crossed the line, I love that he still insists on this passion no matter what. He has, however, learned to make a few concessions when it really counts.

John-Paul (JP) Wollam
Laguna Beach, CA
University of California, Los Angeles, CA

In a Positive Light

It was September 11, 2011, and as typical of the second week of school, I had begun to fall into a daily routine. I woke up at about 6:30 and then sat through my first four classes of the day until lunch. Lunch played out the same and I made my way to 5th period. As I sat there in Mrs. Steele's English class, I expected nothing out of the ordinary review of our hero's journeys we were in the midst of reading.

To my surprise, a call slip was delivered to Mrs. Steele requesting that I bring all my stuff to the office for an appointment. My mind began to wander as I realized I had no appointments or meetings today, and neither my mother nor my father had consulted me on behalf of any plans.

Curiously, I entered the office to find my pastor waiting for me. He appeared dejected, and when he told me that we were headed to the hospital, my mind soared over all the causes for a trip to such a place.

It had been nearly three months since we found out that my dad had a large malignant brain tumor. Our hopes were high and my dad's beaming confidence contributed. He constantly reminded me through all his chemotherapy and surgery that he would come out on top and win.

But suddenly, all that support vanished as I stood looking at my dad in the hospital. He had slipped into a coma that morning and had been rushed to the hospital and put on a ventilator. I sat there looking at him and I couldn't imagine what it would be like to lose a father, to lose my father. Twenty-four hours later we took him off the ventilator, and my life was never the same.

Fortunately, my pain was outweighed by the values he taught me, values that were so deeply engrained in my father's character. Integrity, compassion, and respect were all morals that my dad so greatly inspired within his children and those he met. These values came to represent what people remembered of him, and it guided the way they carried out their own lives.

As for me, my dad's funeral made me think of my own life and how others will remember me. But the more I thought about it, the more I realized that it wasn't just about how people remembered me when I die; it mattered how each person I interacted with remembered me. It shaped the way I treated each individual, regardless of whether I knew him or not.

This outlook certainly does not come easy, but it is an important view of mine that will continue to influence my identity. I wish to be remembered in a positive light, so that everyone that comes into my life, whether it be a store clerk, a high school friend, or a girlfriend, always walks away remembering me for the positive values that I embrace.

ANALYSIS: *I don't believe I helped JP very much at all with this essay, if at all. As you can see, he directly and honestly shared how the news of his dad's illness and shockingly quick death reached him, and how that felt.*

There's no high drama or even an ounce of self-pity, just a teenage boy showing the reader how that news was delivered and how he had no control over how it went down. Then he picked up the storyline and shared how he realized the one thing he could control—his reaction.

Again, JP explained in direct, clear language his thought process after his dad's passing, and how he decided to change how he related with the world. To me, you have no doubt that JP will always view the world in a positive light— no matter how dark it might seem.

Sarah Sandler
Laguna Beach, CA
Saddleback University, Mission Viejo, CA

Sisters Forever

While waiting for our pancakes and eggs to arrive at the local IHOP recently, my little sister decided to pick up one of her crayons and toss it at me. Instead of hitting me, it flew past the side of my head and hit a man sitting behind us at another table.

My sister's blue eyes flew open. Fortunately, the man didn't seem to notice, but we both doubled over laughing. We buried our mouths in our sleeves so no one would hear.

It was just one of the typical silly moments that we have shared together since I first met Julianna almost six years ago. She is the daughter of my mom's longtime boyfriend. Even though she is four years younger than me, we hit it off the first time we met. I even call her my sister.

She lived down in Carlsbad, which is about an hour away, so I saw her about every other weekend or so. We loved going to the movies, and saw one almost every Saturday night. We always loaded up with popcorn and candy and shared it easily. Sometimes we went shopping together. We even went on family vacations together.

No matter what we did, we always had fun. It seemed like almost anything that happened when we were together was hilarious. Like the time we were waiting outside a dressing room for Julianna's older sister, talking to her through the door, and then the door opened and it was a total stranger. We had to leave the store we were laughing so hard!!

Not everyone would get our jokes or silly sense of humor. But having her as my friend and sister means the world to me. I have two brothers, one older and one younger, and always wanted a sister.

So when my mom and her boyfriend decided to split up earlier this year, I was really sad. I knew that it would be hard to spend as much time with Julianna and her older sister, Katherine. But I'm determined to keep our close relationship. We will still be sisters no matter what.

We still talk on the phone and text every day. We bug our parents to make plans so we can get together on weekends. I even have the option to take the train down by myself to see her.

The way I look at friendship is no matter what tries to get in the way, I won't let it happen. I will try my best to keep the connection and find ways to stay in touch and spend time together. To me, having a friend, especially one who feels like a sister, is one of the most important things in my life.

ANALYSIS: Like many students, Sarah insisted she didn't have anything exciting or impressive to write about herself. I had known Sarah since seventh grade, and knew this wasn't true.

After brainstorming ideas, we kept coming back to her family, and how much fun she had with her "sister." One of Sarah's best qualities is that she has a great, fun-loving attitude and enjoys people in general.

At first she didn't think being "loving" and "social" was an important enough quality to impress colleges, but she helped think of real-life moments when she had a good time with her "sister."

Her anecdote grabbed the reader because most of us have had a similar experience like that, where we are messing around with a friend, get in a little trouble, and can't stop laughing.

Caden Robinson
Laguna Beach, CA
University of Puget Sound, Tacoma, WA

The Next Best Thing

For the last six months, I carried around a broken cell phone. One of the two screens refused to turn on, while the other had a black stripe down the center. When reading text messages, I could only guess the words in the middle section. Although once a state-of-the-art phone, my beat-up, two-year-old EnV Touch also had the tendency to "butt dial" random friends.

My old phone reminded me daily of my relentless struggle with technology: I constantly longed for the latest, greatest gadget that promised to change my life, but at the same time I knew if I waited there would always be something better. Was it time to update my computer, camera, cell phone or iPod, or would a newer, better, faster, slimmer device come out in the future that would make my choice obsolete?

Unwilling to risk plunking down my hard-earned cash for a gadget that could be deemed outdated within weeks, I waited. And waited. To console my longing, I drooled over the new devices raved about on tech blogs, such as Gizmodo and Engadget.

My passion for gadgets started when a presenter visited my elementary school to show off the amazing, "game-changing" Windows XP. I envied the advancements, such as its multiple accounts and bubbly graphics. After that, I always asked for a new computer for my birthday and Christmas, but never got one. In seventh grade, I inherited my sister's cast-off computer that was bogged down by malicious software. After researching the Internet for ways to speed up my rust-bucket, I tweaked it to run even faster than my sister's new computer.

After that success, I was hooked. I read everything I could find about how to improve my computer, which led me to other gadget information on the Internet. Soon, I was spending hours every day reading blog posts on multiple sites trying to keep up with the news. To get my hands on the newest gadgets, I would bug my friends to let me play with their latest techie toys to relieve my urge to buy.

I would even pester my mom to drive me to the nearest Apple store so I could mess around with the latest iPod. In my junior year of high school, I wanted a Mac but could not afford one. So I made one. I bought a $300 netbook and scoured online forums to track down the drivers to make it perform like a Mac. It had a few flaws, but worked well and saved me a thousand dollars.

Since then, I continue to make the best of what I have, including my cell phone. It finally died, but instead of investing in a new phone before I'm ready, I bought one used over Ebay. There will always be that pull between what you want, what you can and can't have, and what you just have to accept.

I find that seeking information and improving what I have helps relieve my technology obsession. I am proud of my passion for gadgets, and my drive to understand and improve them. But in the future, I don't want to just wait for the next best thing, I hope to be part of the team that designs and builds it.

ANALYSIS: This was one of my son's core essays. At first, he didn't want my help. But then he had trouble coming up with a topic and let me brainstorm with him. He's always been a "math/science" guy, and was passionate about technology. But what do you write your essay about?

I knew he was obsessed with gadgets, and read all the blogs on the current trends and loved all the techie toys—from video games to his cell phone. But when we thought about it, we realized he always had an outdated phone. That seemed ironic (not what you would expect), and we explored the reason for that.

With these essays, it helps to have something "unexpected" or a twist in your story. This irony seemed like a good one. Once he talked about the funny reason behind his out-of-date phone, he recognized a strong topic.

When he explained this twist on his gadget passion in his essay, Caden also revealed his intense love of technology— all in a natural, funny and personal way. This is exactly what you want in an essay! So keep on the lookout for "twists," or something people wouldn't expect about you, when searching for your own topics.

Sarita Chiu
Phillipines
Smith College, Northampton, MA

Driven

"Para po sa tabi! (Please pull over!)*"*

But the jeepney driver couldn't hear me over the bass.
"Dugz, dugz, dugz," the speakers went, causing the floor and
seats to vibrate. With its purple and green ceiling lights
blinking, the long vehicle sped along like a moving disco,
halting every 20 seconds before speeding away again at 60
km/hr.

"Para po!"

I couldn't see the landmarks outside. The long windows on
either side of the jeepney were blocked by the heads and
shoulders of 20 passengers, crowded in two long seats
meant for 16. "Oh no," I thought. "Did I miss my stop?"

"PARA!"

"Para!" said the woman beside me, but the vehicle
continued. She noticed my panic, banged on the ceiling and
finally caught the driver's attention. The jeepney pulled over.
I smiled my thanks and made my way down the open back,
tripping as it sped off. Relieved that I was safely on the
sidewalk, I soon realized I was nowhere near my school.

The jeepney, an elongated vehicle fabricated from the
original WWII American military jeep, is a cheap and
convenient mode of transportation. Lavishly decorated and

colorfully painted, they have become icons of Philippine culture.

I was scared of jeepneys, let alone riding one by myself. They are terrifyingly fast, sometimes fast enough to send people rolling out. They stop in the middle of the street for passengers, honking and causing heavy traffic jams. Pickpockets sometimes prey on passengers as well.

It was the colorful painted sides of that particular jeepney that determined my first solo ride. I had picked the prettiest among those parked, not knowing it had the loudest speakers or the most number of passengers. "Public transportation lesson number one: No more disco rides," I mumbled and smiled, embarrassed at my poor judgment.

Just then I spotted other students, some younger than me, expertly boarding and alighting from jeepneys that passed me by as I walked the last kilometer to school. My cheeks reddened. "You'll get there. Just a few more rides, and you'll get the hang of it," I consoled myself.

But a few rides weren't enough. I lost track of how many times I got off the wrong street, gave the wrong fare, and rode jeepneys plying the wrong route. On rainy days I tripped over commuters' feet while unintentionally dousing them with rainwater from my umbrella. Once, to the amusement of a full jeepney, I fell off its seat and slipped onto its muddy, wet floor when a passenger forced her generous rump into the already crowded bench.

Nevertheless, I was determined to become an expert. Soon I noticed passengers gave me understanding smiles when I apologized for my clumsiness. I discovered that holding the ceiling handles with my palms out helped prevent numbness, and that sitting directly behind the driver allowed him to hear my *"Para!"* while giving me a better view of landmarks from the vehicle's front windows. And I mastered folding my umbrella neatly while squeezing my behind into crowded seats.

Growing up with very little public transportation experience, I used to be scared of not having my parents drive me around. But after riding different jeepneys with its different passengers, I realized change was exciting, even surprisingly pleasant. Jeepney paintings—ranging from sunsets to profiles of Wolverine— now amuse me.

The passengers—vendors carrying baskets of sticky rice, housewives with dripping bags of fish, students cramming assignments, friendly commuters and rude ones—give me a feeling of belonging. I've found comfort in its stuffy, humid environment I used to despise.

I have yet to learn more about being an adult, and to master riding this vehicle is one small step in that direction. This may seem trivial to others, but for me, it is a rite of passage. To conquer my fear of the speeding, noisy, and overwhelmingly cramped jeepney is a small but significant measure of independence.

Francis Mejia
Dominican Republic
Indiana University Bloomington, IN

The Day I Bullied My Mother

While lying on my bed watching T.V. one night, I thought I had a brilliant idea. I jumped up and walked into my mom's room, where she was sitting on a couch. We could hear my little brother, Osvaldo, playing Playstation in his room down the hall.

"Mom, could you please order us a pizza?" I asked. I couldn't remember the last time we had our favorite, pepperoni and double cheese.

"PIZZA!" my brother shouted from his room, and even left his game to wait for her answer.

My mother looked up at us hovering over her, and said in a soft voice: "Francis, you know I don't have money to buy junk food."

Slightly annoyed, I raised my voice and started to blame her for not having a job. For "sitting in her room doing nothing every day." But after hearing all my accusations, my mother with a dismal look on her face started explaining how hard she was trying to get a job. But angry as a raging bull who saw red, I quickly walked away from her room, ignoring every single word that came out of her mouth.

My father left the house when I was a little kid, too young to understand, too young to miss. I was raised by my single mother for many years until she married again in 2003. But three years after her marriage my stepfather suddenly died from a brain attack. My mother was really hurt inside but her eagerness to work and never back down regardless of the situation was my reason to smile. However things changed when she broke her ankle and was forced to remain in bed for over a year. This injury caused her to lose her job.

Not having a job is no reason to make another person feel bad. In hindsight, it seems like I took all the frustration I had with my father because of his absence in my life and threw it all over my mother. I spent days angry at myself because I couldn't understand how could I blame my mother for something so dense; for not having a job. But this problem was not just between my mother and me. What about my brother? What example am I giving to him? And the fact that my anger was triggered because of a pizza was even worst. I felt weak. I couldn't even talk. Not a word.

Moments such as those made me the person I'm today. No, I'm not perfect, in fact I'm full of flaws, but the way I see and approach others has changed. Sometimes I used to go to places and rarely greeted people, maybe because I was a little shy. In contrast, now every time I see someone, from the supermarket cashier to the bus driver, I try to make some contact to make them feel more comfortable regardless of their social status or situation.

However my mother never let me down. It seemed like she didn't care about all those words I threw at her. Because after that day she was still there. She was still there preparing me breakfast every morning. She was still there asking me how I felt every day after school. But at that moment I was too blind inside my head to realize what her actions really meant. She showed me how to forgive others and live on without hate.

Nathan Selinger
Skokie, Illinois
Northwestern University, Evanston, IL

The Kiss

"Um, now?" I asked the director, praying he was joking.

"Yes." He wasn't.

"Like, on her lips?"

"M-hm."

By now, I have had many "transitions to adulthood." My grandma lovingly shows her friends photos of me chanting Hebrew at my Bar Mitzvah. My closet is stuffed with the blue polos I wore to my first summer job. And I have finally mastered the art of looking cool while driving my little sister around in my mom's red 2001 Dodge Caravan.

However, the community in which I feel I've gained true grown-up status is Thespian Troupe #113, the nationally recognized theatre group at my high school. Nearly twenty hours a week, eight shows a year, and countless late nights memorizing lines or analyzing scripts, my friends and I take pride in putting on professional-quality shows that push the boundaries of what high school theatre can be.

Whether I've been cowering from an onstage school shooting (with a frighteningly realistic gun), showering glitter onto a childhood beauty pageant, or twerking to an all-male a cappella version of "My Milkshake," every show I've worked on has exposed me to new, fascinating challenges. If I had to choose one particular show that marked my theatre "transition to adulthood," it would be when, my sophomore year, I unexpectedly landed a leading role in the fall play—and had to kiss a girl, onstage, for the very first time.

I stood in the rehearsal room, completely flummoxed. I looked at my scene partner, a good-looking junior named Lena who had played the exotic dancer in the previous year's production of RENT. I took a deep breath, puckered up, closed my eyes, and gave her a hurried half-second mouth-touch. The room went quiet.

"We'll work on it later," said the director, clearly unimpressed. My face had turned redder than the small smudge of Lena's lipstick that was now on my lower lip. I quickly turned the page in my script and nervously continued the scene.

Now, if this were an offbeat indie rom-com, the story would go a little like this: Using my awkward boyish charms, I (played by Michael Cera) seduce Lena (Zooey Deschanel) into overlooking my awful kissing and starting an adorably quirky romance with me. The truth, though, gets a little uglier.

As the rehearsals went by, the director's notes went from polite ("Pretend you do this every day") to painfully direct ("Stop looking like you're molesting her!"). This kind of criticism was something completely new to me.

My academic classes got tough at times, but there was always an emphasis on positive feedback and simply "doing your best." In rehearsals, though, the final product was more important than the process. It didn't matter that I was trying my best, since my best attempt at kissing still wasn't good enough for a professional-level show.

My cast mates grew even more impatient. I could tell from their expressions after one particularly disastrous attempt that they were starting to smell my blood in the air. Actually, it was probably Lena's blood in the air, since I had somehow cut her lip with my freshly tightened braces. Hopelessness was setting in. Could I ever get it right?

Finally, it was show time. We had only run the whole thing a handful of times before. Backstage, my knees trembled with anticipation. I can't really remember what happened onstage—it's a panicked blur in my head—but as we took our curtain call, the audience jumped to their feet with applause. We had done it.

I've made many more memories in the theatre department, but this one will always hold a special place in my heart as the time when I began my journey to becoming a theatre grown-up. I'll always cherish the lessons my friends and teachers in theatre have taught me, starting with the universal truth that if at first you don't succeed, just pucker up and try again.

Cassandra Pruitt
Syracuse, NY
Williams College, Williamstown, MA

The Gift

Christmas day at my grandparents' country house, an elegant pink brick building, once a Quaker meetinghouse, nestled in pristine snowy fields. Inside, a fire blazes merrily in the hearth. Stockings droop, overflowing with chocolate, marzipan, truffles, and trinkets. The tree glimmers with ornaments.

Everything is candlelight, old wood and the smell of cloves. The elegant banisters and chandeliers are draped with yards of evergreen garlands. Christmas carols drift from an unseen stereo on the balcony. All around me is Limoge china, gleaming silver, beautiful antiques, blown-glass ornaments, and *tarte tatin*.

My eight-year-old self sits sprawled on the soft Oriental rug in my new Christmas pajamas, surrounded by relatives and mounds of expensive wrapping paper. Presents are given and received, all day. More and more, so many that they cannot be counted: first edition books, cashmere sweaters, collectible dolls, a tiny aquarium, soaps from France, toys from museums. Nothing is enough.

Perhaps, over the years, I've gilded this memory, lingered over the smell of warming *Stollen*. But I've never forgotten the feeling that for all its glossy perfection and elaborate preparation, this day is only an empty box wrapped in beautiful paper. Unspoken words pile in snowdrifts and resentments hang in the air with the scent of pine and nutmeg. What this charming vignette doesn't show is the anxiety beneath the surface, the forbidden sadness, the demand that everything must appear absolutely perfect, no matter the cost.

My childhood was punctuated by these holidays of "wretched excess," as my mother jokingly called them. But life with my mother and sister was fun and spontaneous. After school we explored the forests, gorges and waterfalls of Ithaca. We never had a television; every evening we read together, curled up on our tattered yellow love seat. We played board games and visited museums.

One winter we used no electricity after nightfall, relying on oil lamps and candles to illuminate our evening piano practice. We grew vegetables in our small backyard and painted birdhouses to hang among the flowers. We perused the OED for new words, then made up definitions for them (scopula: a female scallop).

At holidays, instead of shopping, we baked the dozen kinds of Christmas cookies collected in our much-annotated cookbook. We were never wealthy but we were comfortable and happy. I cherished my home life, and the Montessori school we struggled to afford. I had no idea how quickly I could lose these gifts I took for granted.

You know the people you see pushing shopping carts along the highway? That's my family today. We're the ones who have to put groceries back at the checkout because we don't have enough money. This year I'm making do with the remnants of old notebooks because we can't afford new school supplies. I come home to an empty house furnished only with air mattresses and stacks of books.

We have no kitchen; all our food is made with a toaster oven and plug-in kettle perched on a cardboard box. The windowpanes are cracked and I study by the light of a bare bulb. Seven months ago, our ancient car broke down for the last time. Since then, we've been walking or taking the public bus.

You must be wondering how this could have happened. When I was thirteen, my mother's partner left without a backward glance, leaving behind his Steelers coffee mug and his business debts; the next year my loving grandfather died with an expired will; and my mother's health problems worsened, leaving her chronically bedridden. In addition to drastic material loss, these momentous changes stripped away my sense of safety and continuity. Untethered from everything that had defined my life, I didn't feel at home anywhere. I was living on a knife's edge.

It took years, but when my life finally settled into a new shape, despite the countless losses, I had gained unimaginable resilience and perspective. Poverty entails a thousand petty humiliations, but it has also stripped away the nonessential, imparting clarity and uncovering deeper values. We chose to sell our antique silver in order to keep driving the long commute to school. We chose to sell clothes instead of books, our furniture, but not the piano. Looking around this room, everything I see is precious to me: my books, my flute, my running shoes, my schoolwork, my beloved dog, my mug of tea.

Equally valuable are my newly developed resourcefulness and perseverance, the new closeness with my little family and my evolving gratitude.

I see my past clearly for what it was— the rich opportunities, the glow of security, as well as the dependence on surface perfection. I also see the present, with its unexpected joys and its refrain of uncertainties. Each morning I wake up to unanswered questions, but I feel at home in myself and in my life.

Please note: this essay was submitted for QuestBridge, an organization that helps match high-achieving, low-income students with top colleges, hence the 800-word count.

Eleasha Chew
Penang, Malaysia
Harvard University, Boston, MA

Overflow

I have always been mesmerized by water.

When I was 8, I would often wait for my parents to pick me up by a little drain next to my primary school. As queer as it may seem, I loved watching the rivulets of drain water flowing past, especially when they caught the golden flecks of evening sunlight and shimmered like scattered sequins. They always brought to mind the gurgling brooks in Montgomery's 'Anne of Green Gables'. I was smitten and adopted the drain as my very own gurgling brook.

When I was 17 and preparing for a month of intense national examinations, I eagerly welcomed the rain. When it did rain, I would slip out to the balcony, dragging with me a white stool and my revision books. This was when I learned best, with the glorious view of rainwater slipping off the roof in torrents and the spray of dancing raindrops upon my face.

As I soon discovered, water watching is an art. Magic happens whenever I watch water from the perfect distance – far enough to watch as it ripples, leaps and sparkles, but near enough to hear its joyful bubbling and the humming of air all around. My worries and fears melt away, and I begin to come alive.

These magical moments became so valuable to me that I began to consciously seek them out. To my delight, I learned that this magic transcends borders. I came alive at the sight of the turquoise waters of the Bosphorus, wind rushing through my hair as I leaned over the railing of the ship deck. I came alive gazing at the rolling waves of the Pacific Ocean, the vast expanse of gemstone-blue waters kissing the skies at the horizon. I came alive as I beheld the grace with which

135

water rippled over the lily pad-covered ponds of Angkor Wat. I came alive as I stood, awed by the waterfall I stumbled upon in Penang, waters leaping off the precipice and tumbling into the foaming ecstasy-pool below.

I often ask myself, what exactly is it about watching water that captivates and enlivens me? I wonder if it has to do with my deep-set conviction that there can be beauty and an inherent goodness in every circumstance, and that the struggle to seek out the beauty in everything, while difficult, is completely worthwhile.

In all my years of water watching, the motion of water speaks to me of one thing – rapture at the miracle of life. It may be water droplets dripping from eaves or water currents swishing over rocks but water always seems to me as quivering with pure bliss, reveling fully in the joy of its existence. This rejoicing is contagious. Watching water reminds me of how I want to live my life—eyes wide open, embracing every moment, constantly filled with wonder at the privilege of being alive.

Yet, water watching is not merely a reminder of an ideal attitude towards life – it is also my means to that end. It allows me to step away from the endless rushing around, to slow time down by being completely immersed in little wonders, like how falling raindrops form ripples, concentric circles puffing out and disappearing. It convinces me that the struggle to hold on to the beautiful amidst the mess and the brokenness is worthwhile, for even in the encompassing darkness of night, water stubbornly chooses to catch on to the faintest specks of light, replacing the dark emptiness with something beautiful.

I may never truly know why being around water is so significant to me, but what I do know is that it has shown me how our lives have been graced with infinite beauty, and that the only appropriate response is overflowing gratefulness.

Andrew Yang
Eden Prairie, MN
University of Illinois, Champagne, IL

Scratch Guru

Crayons, construction paper, calculator: I head over to a corner and set these supplies down. Then, I let my mind wander. The school year has recently started, and I know absolutely nobody because I have recently switched schools.

Making new friends hasn't been easy because I am perhaps the only boy in the class who doesn't idolize Kobe. Coupled with my disinterest in girls' cooties, I have found it easier to head to my corner and pursue my solitary ventures.

I refocus on the task at hand: devising math problems and solving them. Letting the magic of numbers conquer my mind, I robotically mumble, "Sixteen plus seventeen equals thirty-three. Eleven times eight equals eighty-eight." My crayon translates my words onto the paper like clockwork. Then, I feel a hand on my shoulder.

Surprised, I turn around to see an old man who could have been in an old Western movie. After the initial greetings, I show him my math skills on the sheet of construction paper. As my hand moves, the numbers transport both of us into a trance, and as I devise and solve the problems, he nods and smiles in approval.

"You're really good at math," he acknowledges.

"Th-th-th-thank you," I stammer. The excitement of being complimented overwhelms my first-grade mind. I eagerly dive right back into the realm of numbers and let its spell overcome my brain.

In front of my computer screen, I watch my platforming game unfold. While my classmates were playing fantasy football or watching the Vikings game, I start to debug my project. I press the right arrow key. Satisfied with the result, I press up to jump. Boing! Satisfied with the physics, I pump my fist. My creation has come to fruition.

At the beginning of eighth grade, I saw some of my friends gathered around a computer. On the computer screen, a cartoon cat moved around by these things called "scripts," which looked like a tower of digital Lego blocks. And there was an entire arsenal of different Lego blocks that did different tasks. The program's name was called "Scratch."

A week later the geometry teacher assigned a programming assignment. The software of choice: Scratch. Once I returned to my computer, I immediately downloaded this program and started tinkering around. Realizing that I could add and replace the moving computer images called "sprites," I replaced the Scratch cat with Mario.

Dismayed that Mario can go through walls and that his jumps don't look realistic according to the laws of physics, I toiled to implement basic collision detection and gravity. Staying up to midnight didn't please Mother, but tinkering with virtual Lego blocks captivated me. The realm of programming logic has a firm grip on my mind, and it refuses to let go.

The next day in class, I show my classmates the game. Amazed, they dub me the "Scratch Guru." Even the teacher checks my game out; he plays it on his laptop for the entire class period. During that time my classmates begin to ask me for help.

Soon, I find joy in helping other people with their problems. With each question from a fellow classmate, I walk us through the magic of the virtual blocks, leaving the classmate awestruck and leaving me more confident. With each patching of malfunctioning scripts, I raise my voice louder and louder, making it easier for classmates to hear me. And with each fix of a physics bug, I make more and more acquaintances, and even some friends. As the bell rings, I finish helping my friend fix some bugs. After rearranging the blocks, he tests his project. He presses the spacebar. The stick figure on the screen performs a jump that follows a perfect parabolic trajectory.

Smiling, he turns to me and says, "You're really good at programming!"

Annie Beier
Sandy Hook, CT
Brown University, Providence, RI

I Scream For Ice Cream

I used to struggle with questions like "AP Gov or AP Econ?" and then all of a sudden, my head was flooded with questions like "Cow Trax, Campfire, or Bada Bing?"

Starting my job at Newtown's iconic Ferris Acres Creamery ushered me into a whole new world full of "creative" flavor combinations, some VERY regular customers, and sprinkles that find their way into every nook and cranny of the building. Add in a persistent aroma of cow manure, and you've arrived at the locally-owned, picturesque little barn that is my home away from home.

Let me just say that working at this ice cream shop is definitely harder than it looks, or at least harder than I ever imagined. It's like a walk in the park, if your park is really an obstacle course that includes exploding hot fudge machines, volcanic milkshakes, and lifting an infinite number of 2.5 gallon ice cream tubs. My arms constantly ached for my first month on the job. Every shift I met new challenges, whether it was a register code I didn't know, a flavor frozen harder than concrete, or the need to force a polite smile the 200th time someone used the gag name "Batman" to pick up their order.

My first obstacle was the oh-so-temperamental soft serve machine. As an experienced consumer of self-serve frozen yogurt, I didn't take it very seriously when the other employees told me how difficult the machine was to operate. I even remember thinking to myself, "Yikes, have none of these people ever been to FroyoWorld?" But then it was just me and the machine—the massive, humming, and (here's the kicker) pressurized machine.

As it turns out, pressurized actually means that as soon as the lever is pulled down to a certain point, ice cream comes spewing out with ridiculous speed. I learned the hard way how quickly it could go from letting nothing out to expelling enough vanilla soft serve to overfill my very small cup by about six quarts. This stainless steel beast dwarfed me in its shadow as I tried to position the lever to the exact millimeter to avoid another disaster. Even when I finally won a battle, I knew I was a long way from winning the war.

There's something about this job that is just so special to me, despite the many times I've spilled ice cream all over my clothes or ruined a great hair day by bunning-up with a hairnet and hat. It's a treat to see the inner workings of an incredibly well-run small business that creates success through quality products, hard work, and the remarkable ability to keep a staff of 50 teenagers in line.

I feel a huge sense of pride when I wear my Creamery sweatshirt, which on the back advertises our shop as "Where the Cows Cross" (referring to the crossing of cows across state highway 302 from the barn to the grazing fields—a big hit for preschoolers, and my mom, but not so much for commuters).

I think what I love so much about it is how much I've learned since I've started working there, and also how much I know I've yet to learn. There's just something so refreshing about always making new little discoveries, like where we keep the extra cherries or what's on a Turtle Sundae. But I've also discovered something much bigger—the importance of going out of my comfort zone, seeking new opportunities, being a good team member, and staying determined to succeed, no matter how many cows are blocking the path to success.

Hebani Duggal
Milford, CT
Cornell University, Ithaca, NY

Piping Up

I was in the second grade when I first learned what the middle finger meant. It was my first week in the United States, and a boy with bright eyes and chubby hands was trying to be social in the lunchroom. He walked out of line, sat down next to me, and pulled the one finger out of his pocket, asking me if I wanted to "see something cool". He managed to wave it around for about four minutes before an alarmed teacher pulled him away.

I couldn't wait to show my parents when I got home. To say they were alarmed would be to say the World Wars were mild conflicts. My parents were terrified. Their daughter, the girl who'd learned to speak English before Hindi in Mumbai, the girl who'd slaughtered three lizards a day in their home in Singapore, the girl who'd bowed to every Buddha statue she could find in Japan, had learned how to swear in America. It was safe to say my parents were nervous about my future in this country.

They really had no reason to worry. Learning what the middle finger meant my first few days in this country was the best experience I could've had. In that one moment, I had been introduced to the American ideal that would shape my identity the most – the power of expression.

Fresh out of living in countries like India and Singapore where societies are centered on what students should say and how students should behave, I came to America a shy, rather quiet girl. My mind was filled with ideas, my eyes took in every sight, and my brain tucked away every notable experience – I just never expressed them. I'd been taught and trained to take in an education, but I'd never learned to

142

use an education. As I became more accustomed to this new country, I observed America as an environment that valued wielding an opinion over simply gaining knowledge.

This observation only grew stronger as I climbed higher up in my education. There were a few modifications, of course–I realized expressions of passionate beliefs are generally appreciated more if they're educated rather than rude. The emphasis placed on forming ideas and expressing them began to have a significant impact on me. I found myself piping up to share my opinions in my classes and questioning ideas not only at school, but at home as well (a change my parents were a bit less enthusiastic about).

America was bold, and I began to match its boldness. I sauntered into school the day after the Arizona Immigration laws hit the headlines and simmered in my classes, speaking my mind and finding others to play devil's advocate. My essays took the side of troubled countries over powerful ones. I proceeded to (respectfully) disagree with my teachers from time to time – and further terrify my parents.

Occasionally, when I mull over the memories I link to each country I've lived in, I immediately associate America with the first time I learned what the middle finger meant. I think back to that experience, and I think about what the middle finger means to me. Profanities aside, the middle finger stands as the part of America that tugged at my passions and pushed me to express them. As I look towards an education that continues to shape my identity, the little boy and his finger represent the part of me that chooses to no longer remain silent about the world around me.

Amelia Karlin
Barrington, Rhode Island
The University of Pennsylvania, Philadelphia, PA

How Do You Feel About That?

I confess, "My dad is a psychiatrist, my mom is a psychologist." At this point, new acquaintances pause in conversation and hushed murmurs of sympathy are offered my way. Perhaps others begin to suspect what I already know – I was raised with questions, many questions: "Why did you say this? What was going through your mind? What was your intention?" And, of course, the ultimate, the dreaded, parent- therapist query: "And, how do you feel about that?"

My parents value introspection and self-awareness. To some degree I do too, but, sometimes, as a busy 17- year-old high school senior, I just want to get through the day on autopilot. The constant inquiries can irritate; they interrupt my flow. My response, admittedly, is not always optimal.

And, yet, I am the one in the front of the room, falling off the chair, hand flying in the air – "Pick me, pick me!" I do not want to blurt out the answer, I want to ask the next question. Questions offer a glimpse into the unknown, so why not ask them? I recognize that I risk public humiliation and that my questioning can be seen as excessive ("Yes, what now Mimi?"). I am learning to temper myself, but if the truth be told, only so much.

Perhaps the question gene is dominant in my family DNA; perhaps I am a product of my environment. Most likely, both are true. Whatever the case, I will be the first to admit that I too live to question.

For me, questions are not so much about the self-analysis so dear to my parents. I value insight into the ways of the world. I realize that I have a strong need to understand the

144

"how" and the "why". I need to know details in order to grasp the bigger picture and I tend to feel uncomfortable with incomplete knowledge. If I know the facts, then I can be correct, but when I fully grasp the concept, I am at ease. When I understand, I am able to use my knowledge – I am able to retain and recall, but better yet, apply what I now know.
And then, inevitably, I can ask more questions...

My curiosity has become a defining personality characteristic and I hope to use it positively. When I contemplate a future in health care, my inquisitive nature will be an asset. Ever since early childhood I have had a fascination with the human body. I have been a case study of one: I have been known to exaggerate the slightest twinge of discomfort in order to engage my physician-father in a "why/what/how" conversation on the workings of the body. My obsession to understand the symptom will lead me to the bigger picture of diagnosing the disease.

As I mature I am beginning to realize that this form of understanding, by itself, is not enough. As a compassionate caregiver, I will need to know more. Somehow, I no longer resent my parents' ultimate question and have come to appreciate its value. I look forward to asking my patients the question: "How do you feel?" Only by listening closely to the answer will I truly begin to understand. My parents taught me well.

Martina Pansze
Durango, Colorado
Whitman College, Walla Walla, WA

Taming The Beast

A green Ford Bronco has hunkered in a back corner of our driveway for as long as I can remember. It stood steadfast through searing sun and hood-high blizzards, and for a while it complacently hosted a raccoon family inside its grimy stomach. It was my dad's old car, and to him it was a fond trophy of nostalgia. The seat was frayed not by the backsides of jeans, but by the weight of thick memories.

To me, it looked like the rusty ruin of an atomic explosion. Flecks of paint had spewed from the car to cover the pavement like autumn leaves. A crack spider-webbed across the windshield and a small forest ensnared the wipers. We called it "The Beast." I once asked my dad why he didn't sell it for parts, or more realistically, drop it off at the junkyard. To my dismay, he responded, "Then what would you drive?"

Oh no. I had imagined my first car to be much more…intact.

Despite my prayers, when the time came for me to sit in the driver's seat, The Beast was deemed sufficiently alive. I was thrust quite unwillingly into the challenge of backing out of the driveway, and mine is not your average suburban driveway. Our house gets no visitors on Halloween; no kid is willing to make the trek. Years ago I used to ski down it, making laps again and again until the pavement poked through the snowpack and my gloves were stiff with ice. But today it was July, and my skis lay forgotten deep in a closet.

My mom gave me a short lesson on the pedals, and with some perseverance the engine finally awoke: first with a groan, and then with a roar. I took a breath and anchored my hands at ten and two o'clock on the shuddering, lopsided

146

wheel. Brake, clutch all the way in, gear in reverse, ease the gas pedal down slowwwlllllyyy.

We immediately shot backwards as if flung from a slingshot. In the jolt, my left foot had slipped off the pedal. Luckily in the face of chaos, I am gifted with the ability to ground my mind and find reason.

I prepared myself for action and let go of the steering wheel in a desperate panic while accidentally stomping the gas pedal. Within a few yards we had inelegantly smashed into oak branches. "That tree needed to be trimmed," my mom said graciously.

But her forgiveness was not reassuring. I was quite certain that I could never tame The Beast. It would be less stressful and more time-efficient to put the car in neutral and hire somebody to push it. I circled the neighborhood, but I didn't seem to make any progress and this exasperated me to no end. I grew increasingly anxious and frustrated. The hours I spent behind the wheel became few and far between. A few months later I decided to give it another chance. I was surprised when the pedals felt familiar, and I turned the ignition with a shred of newfound confidence.

Sure enough, The Beast kindly avoided branched obstacles this time. On my neighborhood route I stalled only thrice and was honked at just once, a personal record. Jerking to a halt in the driveway, I felt a rush of pride. One of the many, many miles on the odometer was all my own!

Seeing the results of my work justified my previous frustration, and I realized I shouldn't quit if I'm not gifted at something new. Doing so is forfeiting the chance to gain a skill or unearth an interest. The Bronco has character in a way I never appreciated and suits me in a way I definitely didn't expect. The Beast and I are a pedestrian-avoiding, stop-light-conquering, pavement-ruling duo. No trees dare to step in our path.

ACKNOWLEDGEMENTS

The Story Behind These Essays

Most of these essays are from my former students, who I tutored either privately or attended my group workshops. You might notice that most of them followed a similar narrative writing format, where they started with an anecdote and continued from there. I believe this is one of the most natural and effective ways to write an engaging essay using storytelling techniques.

Many of these essays were from local students who worked with college admissions consultants based in my hometown of Laguna Beach—Kristin Thomas, who has since moved onto a different career, and Lynn Fair, of Square One—who hired me to help their clients with these essays. They also had guidance from their English teachers, high school counselors, parents, friends, and others.

Both Kristin and Lynn had a big hand in many of these essays, from helping students find topics to proofing their final drafts. It was no coincidence that their young clients consistently landed in top-choice schools, and received acceptance offers and scholarships from many others. We were all convinced narrative-style essays often played a role in their success.

I also included ten essays at the end that were written by students I did not help, at least not directly. The students sent them in for an essay-writing contest that I held on my blog. These are the ones I liked the best, and although most are "narrative," I think they offer some different styles, structures, topics and voices. These students credited everyone—including their parents, teachers, counselors, friends, and yes, even me (via my EssayHell.com blog and guide books). A few said they wrote their essays completely on their own. Bravo!

And I want to thank my own two "children," Cassidy and Caden, who let me help them with their essays during their stressful junior and senior years of high school, even though it felt like torture for them at times. Those early experiences taught me how to leverage real-life stories to make college application essays powerful and effective.

I'm also grateful for Russell Pierce, master graphic designer and Laguna Beach artist, who had enormous patience with me in designing the fun cover for this collection, as well as my other Essay Hell books (*Escape Essay Hell* and *Essay Hell's Prompts Primer*) and my Web site graphics on EssayHell.com.

Finally, a huge Thank You! to the students who gave me permission to share their essays in this collection. Many were highly personal. Some were quite a struggle to get down on paper. I'm grateful for all students who took the time to reflect on their lives and wrestle with words and language to express their ideas, feelings, insights, goals and dreams. Writing is risky. And sharing it often takes courage.

We are the stories we tell. And I'm honored to share these. I hope they inspire you to find and tell yours as well.

Janine Robinson

Made in the USA
San Bernardino, CA
06 June 2018